The
Life
of
Manny

The Life of Manny

Discovering Why People Follow A Leader

RAY EAST

Horizon East • New York

The Life of Manny: Discovering Why People Follow a Leader
© 2010 by Raymond G. East

Published by Horizon East, Inc.

101 West 23rd Street
Suite 715
New York, NY 10011

www.HorizonEast.info

Library of Congress Control Number: 2009923931
ISBN: 978-09823555-4-1

Category: Leadership/Management

Book cover and interior design by www.KarrieRoss.com

You may purchase copies of this book at a discount when ordered in quantity
for bulk purchases or special sales. For more information, please visit our
website: www.TheLifeofManny.com

Printed in the United States of America
First Printing 2010

Dedicated to

Lois M. East

I love you, Picky-Head LoLo.

CONTENTS

THE STORY

FINAL ITEMS

❖ ❖ ❖

WELCOME

The brightest stars in every field are the people who excel in the basics of their calling. The field of leadership is no different. Unfortunately, vast numbers of leaders today are only vaguely familiar with the basics of good leadership. They don't really know how to be the kind of leaders whom people *want* to follow. They are only weakly competent at arousing initiative and loyalty in others. As a result, many of our families, schools, businesses, nonprofits and governments are in a state of dysfunction.

The greatest leaders in human history all had very different leadership styles, but they all adopted a confident, humble and sometimes subversive way of life. This lifestyle is, without a doubt, the main quality a leader needs to achieve breakthrough results through other human beings. And it can be learned.

The following fictional story is designed to inspire this kind of life in you.

Welcome to The Life of Manny.

PART ONE

❖　　❖　　❖

The Dare

CHAPTER ONE

Over eight million souls vibrated in the City of New York that snowy afternoon. For the first time in years, he was one of them. Manny Johnson stood in LaGuardia Airport, silently willing the conveyor belt to move. Most folks would say he was somewhat handsome but he didn't think much about that. He stood a hair under six feet tall, dressed in khakis and a blue polo shirt even though it was winter.

Manny was absently patting a hand against the side of his pants. He was nervous. The buzzer sounded and the baggage belt lurched forward. Luggage appeared. He raised a bottle of water to his lips and drank. At that moment, someone snuck up behind him and abruptly jumped on his back. Water flew from his bottle—and his mouth—in every direction before the unknown man jumped off.

Startled, Manny turned around and identified the assailant as Jack Jameson, his old business school roommate. Jack was a tall, trim man with a chiseled face and night black hair. They instantly doubled over in laughter. They were still belly laughing a minute later as they wiped the tears from their eyes. Nothing had changed. It was like the good old days back at Columbia University.

Jack regained his composure enough to speak. "You haven't changed at all, Manny." The statement was mostly true, even though a few silver strands had now established themselves throughout Manny's wavy brown hair.

Manny nodded in acknowledgement. "Well, I never thought I'd move back here after graduation. For that matter, I never dreamed I'd be working for you either." A slow grin surfaced. "But here I am!" Manny's golden eyes radiated warmth— especially when he smiled. "So are you ready for my office to be down the hall from yours?"

Jack was one of those busy Type-A executives who was constantly in motion. In fact, by the time Manny finished his sentence, Jack was already halfway through replying to a text message on his Blackberry. He stopped and looked up. "As long as you take me to lunch often and gracefully defer to me in staff meetings, we'll be just fine." He flashed a smile and threatened, "Watch out, world! Jameson and Johnson are together again!"

Manny lived for impromptu moments of shared joy like this. "I'll make you proud," he said. He exhaled deeply and realized there was no reason to be nervous after all. Even though they'd been out of touch with each other for years, they still seemed compatible.

"Did Susan and the kids make it in okay with the snow?" asked Jack.

"Yup. They got in a few hours ago and are getting settled. I had to stick around in Kansas City a little longer and finish the house closing." A blue bag made a slow voyage around the curve of the conveyor belt. Manny stepped forward to grab it. He walked, as usual, with a sense of purpose. He was physically strong for an executive who was almost forty.

Jack was strong too. He jostled Manny out of the way and beat him to the luggage. "I got it," he said, hoisting the bag off the belt.

"Thanks, Jack."

"No problem."

Manny rested his hand on Jack's shoulder. "No, I mean thanks for bringing me here."

"I know."

It was a little past seven on Monday morning when Jack, Manny and Susan walked through the door of Jerry's Diner on West 57th Street. The place had all the signs of a good diner, including chrome décor and the smell of bacon wafting everywhere. The group made their way through the crowd to a red booth in the corner. It was a warm place to flee the winter cold.

Manny and Susan slid into one side of the booth and faced Jack on the other. Manny rested a folded copy of the *New York Times* on the table and smiled at his wife. Susan was a beautiful woman by anyone's account. Brown curls framed her face. She radiated an easygoing strength. Her beauty and smarts blended into a girl-next-door appeal that had swept Manny off his feet fourteen years ago when they met at a carnival. He had known instantly that they were meant to be together, but she hadn't been as sure. When they first met, she gave him the bare minimum attention that courtesy required. But Manny wasn't going to let a little obstacle like that thwart him. He had no choice but to do everything in his power to woo her.

The weeks following the carnival saw chocolates, flowers, a walk in the park, surprise visits at work and a random cigar. He listened to her too. There was lots of listening. She became overwhelmed by the skillful way he cared for her—she began to fear that he was too good to be true. She decided she would take her time and she did, observing Manny's interactions with countless family members, friends and even strangers. Then one day, no more time was needed. It was a done deal.

The waitress now towered over the booth in a stained pink uniform so the three ordered breakfast. Jack asked how Susan's first days negotiating New York City had gone. She spent a few minutes informing him about how the movers had finally arrived from Kansas City with all the furniture and how the kids loved their new bedroom.

Jack placed a napkin on his lap. "Now that you've got your furniture, you'll be feeling settled in no time. There's no other city in the world like New York. Ever since I was in college, I knew I wanted to live in New York City, Tokyo and Hong Kong. I was planning on staying in New York for three years before moving on to Asia, but somehow three years turned into sixteen." He smiled and then noticed the copy of the *Times* on the table. He pointed to an article on the front page. "Did you guys read about the soldier who threw himself over the exploding grenade? Incredible. He saved at least four guys in his unit. It seems like war heroes are in the news a lot these days."

Susan added, "Most of them say they don't really feel like a hero because they were just doing what they knew they had to do for their friends. And they usually say their main motivation for fighting is not their mission or their country. They're fighting to protect the guys next to them."

Jack read on and wondered aloud, "But it says that he'd only been transferred into the platoon a week earlier." Jack couldn't comprehend how this could be. Such an act of bravery seemed too huge a price for a soldier to pay for people he hardly knew.

The waitress poured coffee into Manny's cup. "Thanks." Manny turned to Jack. "When you're in the middle of a war, a week is more than enough time for loyalty to grow. After all, in a situation like that, you find your life from the people at your side."

Jack's brow furrowed. "Find life?"

Manny leaned forward. "Yeah. When I was in the Gulf War, the most loyal friendships grew out of the most intense pressure. Every day in the Marines was a struggle for me... emotionally, physically. I had plenty of time out in the desert every night to ask the real questions: Will my body give out? What if the enemy tortures me? How will my loved ones make it if I don't come home? These things weigh on you."

Susan put a hand on Manny's shoulder. She knew how important this was to him. They'd discussed it countless times before. He smiled and closed his eyes, reflecting on his time in the sand long ago. The times he ate dust, crawling on the ground to evade enemy fire with a heavy load of equipment on his back. The hopeless, lonely times when he felt like giving up. That humble feeling he got when the afflictions of the day tested every ounce of his will to live.

"The guys in my squad poured life into me at my lowest points. We marched together, we shared our hopes and fears and we protected each other. In the middle of the desert, we gave life to each other. It's amazing how quickly loyalty arises under those circumstances."

Manny recalled the face of a scraggly kid named Noah who was one of those brothers in the desert. Long after the war was over, Manny and Noah found themselves bumbling through life together as best friends back in Kansas City. Manny had somehow managed the transition to civilian life when he arrived back home. He got a job at a bank and started dating an attractive girl named Susan. Noah, however, was at a loss when it came to reinventing his life. He lacked a sense of direction.

About a year after Manny and Susan got married, Noah went into a dark depression. He became well known at the local bar where he medicated his pain. Manny took him aside one day and made him talk at length about his sadness. Apparently, Noah had decided to apply to the University of Kansas in Overland Park. He'd been accepted to the school but he didn't have enough money to go, even with the financial aid package the school had offered.

Manny was frustrated that he didn't have enough money to help his friend financially. He brainstormed with Susan later that night and they decided they could help in a non-financial way. They made a quick plan to fix up their extra bedroom so Noah could live rent-free near campus. The two hopped in their blue Honda after dinner and headed to the mall. They bought a desk, a rolling chair and a bookshelf. Noah had tears in his eyes the next day when they showed him his new room and study space. Susan invited him to eat meals with them every day so he could save money on food too. Noah's dream was suddenly within reach.

The next years were hard, but Noah's loans, summer internships and part-time work at a sub sandwich shop provided him just enough money each semester to cover tuition and books. He was holding down a job, making decent grades and, at long last, had a family to live with. Noah was thriving. He found life from a friendship forged in the desert.

The waitress approached the table, impressively balancing three omelette platters on a single arm. Manny opened his eyes. An hour's worth of memories had trekked through his head in just a few seconds.

Jack had a blank look on his face.

Manny decided to wrap things up. "I've discovered that a tightly knit group of soldiers can break through seemingly impossible obstacles to accomplish a mission. <u>Most military units share a strength that corporate work teams never even approach</u>. I'm always looking for ways to bring the best of the desert to bear in the workplace."

Jack buttered his toast and felt a twinge of uneasiness deep within. He couldn't quite put his finger on what was making him feel this way. Was it something about the conversation? Perhaps it was indigestion.

CHAPTER TWO

The sidewalks of Columbus Circle were encased in white, except for the well-trodden, brownish trails of mush, courtesy of the rush-hour crowds. Manny and Jack emerged from the diner and joined the great march of pedestrians plying their way to work. They walked silently under a clouded sky. Manny was feeling the power of the moment to come; he was about to embark on his first day at a prestigious management-consulting firm. Butterflies danced in his stomach.

Jack's thoughts were focused on his most recent job evaluation. "You know, I didn't get the biggest bonus this year. My performance review was great except for the new 'Leadership' section. The associates who report to me all had to anonymously assign scores to rate my leadership abilities. I guess my scores weren't the best."

Manny shuffled around the side of a man to avoid the eight dogs he was holding on leashes. Only in New York, Manny thought. He turned his attention back to Jack. "Sorry to hear that."

"It's alright. I guess busy people like me are just more focused on producing than dealing with people challenges. Anyhow, that's one of the reasons why you're coming on board. I want you to handle the team so I can focus on the bigger stuff. Do you think you can hit the ground running?"

Manny walked a few paces in silence. "I'll do my best, Jack... but I can't tell you what's possible until I get to know the team, the culture, the issues."

"Fair enough."

"What are the main challenges you're facing?"

Jack stopped on the corner. Commuters glided past them in all directions. He smiled. "You just want the top ten or the whole list? It's harder to recruit and maintain associates than ever before. Cyrus & Hopkins attracts talented MBA grads every year with a high need to achieve, yet only a few of them want to stay for a career with the firm. Every year, they have higher expectations of us, but they don't trust us. They're motivated but not loyal to the firm, so they don't stay long. I lost another associate just last week, Pam Weathers, and she was really talented."

Jack continued walking across the street. "Our clients are getting more demanding and expect to pay less. New clients are harder to come by, thanks to the new boutique and mega-firms competing for their attention. Worst of all, I find myself putting out fires rather than focusing on long-term strategy."

Manny's nondescript expression concealed his inner query. What have I gotten myself into? Jack never made the situation sound so bleak before I accepted the job, he thought. This is going to be interesting. And by interesting, Manny meant painful.

They reached a concrete and glass building. Jack passed through the revolving doors first. Manny followed. They trod their feet on the black welcome mat and Jack shed his outer coat, revealing a perfectly tailored charcoal suit and a red tie.

The elevator doors opened to the twenty-fifth floor and they entered the plush lobby of Cyrus & Hopkins, LLP. Expensive artwork adorned the walls and Persian rugs graced the floors. Floor-to-ceiling windows framed the reception foyer. The view of the skyline was appropriately impressive.

Starting with only a handful of colleagues ten years ago, Cyrus & Hopkins had grown steadily into a management consulting firm with sixty-seven professionals. Although they lacked the global reputation and expansive client base of the larger consulting firms, the group was known for their solid impact on their clients' performance levels. The firm had helped companies overcome business challenges in the areas of strategy, marketing, finance and operations. They also did a little work in information technology (IT) consulting.

You've got what it takes, Manny told himself as he strode purposefully to the reception desk and extended his hand to Louise Archer, the woman sitting there. "Hi, I'm Manny Johnson. I'm starting here today," he said in his hello-new-person voice.

Sixteen handshakes later, Manny realized that Jack was leading him to his new office the long way in order to make introductions. Manny had conversations with eight associates, four managers, and three partners. He even met Deborah Hopkins herself, the managing partner. Little by little, with each handshake, his butterflies departed. He at last had faces to put with the names he'd heard over the phone.

Finally, Jack stopped at the threshold of an office so Manny could walk through first. Manny entered and his eyes widened. The space was generously sized, to say the least. A discussion area with chairs, a couch and a coffee table were to the left. An executive desk made of cherry wood and a leather roller chair were to the right. And adjacent to the cherry file cabinets, the room was crowned with a wintry vista of Central Park.

"I'm three doors down." Jack's voice trailed off as he walked toward his office. "Come by once you've settled in."

Manny hadn't seen the firm's offices before. Since Jack's travel schedule had conflicted with his in weeks prior, they'd arranged Manny's interviews over the phone and by videoconferencing. While in Kansas City, he'd envisioned what the office would look like a million times, but he never expected such a lavish setup. He walked around the perimeter of the room and stood in front of the window. This was more than he could have hoped for.

A surge of gratitude and longing seized his heart. He wanted Susan and his children to share the moment with him. He marveled at how Susan had so willingly left her hometown and extended family to move to New York and fulfill his professional dream. He reached for the cell phone in his right pants pocket and called home.

While talking to Susan, he set his briefcase on top of the desk, sat down in the chair and started unpacking. He positioned a thesaurus, financial dictionary and two framed pictures of his family on the desk. One of Susan. One of Samantha and Ryan. He opened the top drawer and was greeted by a sole sheet of paper. It read "Cyrus & Hopkins LLP Staff Telephone Directory" in bold letters on the top along with the firm's understated logo. He searched through the names of the associates under the "Blue Pod" section. These would be his people.

A few minutes later, Jack looked up from the substantial mound of paper on his desk to see Manny walking through his door holding a bottle of water.

Jack split the mountain into two and started to sort through the left pile. "Everything good? Like your space?"

"Perfect." Manny looked around Jack's office and noted that it was even larger than his own and had an extra window. The disparity, naturally, was a function of firm hierarchy. Jack was a partner. Manny had an appropriately smaller office and one less windowpane since he was a manager and still one step away from becoming a partner. At Cyrus & Hopkins, both partners and managers led teams of associates. These teams were formally called pods. Typically a pod would be led by the partner, with one or two managers helping him. The division of labor varied depending on the pod, but generally, the partner's work emphasized rainmaking (acquiring new clients), whereas the manager focused more on coordinating the associates' day-to-day work.

The associates in each pod did most of the actual consulting analysis. They were MBA grads with experience in a variety of industries and functions. Manny was genuinely impressed when he read their firm bios. The associates were supported, in turn, by highly capable administrative staff and a handful of analysts, freshly out of the top colleges.

Each pod was like a mini consulting firm with its own budget and rainmaking initiatives. Specialist consultants were sometimes added to or removed from a pod as a particular case required. The pod arrangement was somewhat special to the firm, and partners made much about the synergy and teamwork made possible by the innovative firm structure.

Jack continued to study his paper mountain. "Could you close the door for a second?"

"Sure." Manny backtracked and shut the door.

"I've scheduled Conference Room B at ten-thirty to introduce you to the pod. They're a solid bunch. You should probably prepare some brief remarks if you haven't done so already."

"No problem. I'm prepared."

"You'll meet Linda Flores there. She's probably the most brilliant strategist on our team and she can multi-task like nobody's business. She could be a real ally for you here, but…" Jack looked up. "You might want to keep your eyes on her. She was the internal candidate for the position you took. She really wanted the position, so… you know how it goes. She may not want to see you succeed as much as I do. In the days ahead, as we meet people, I'll tell you about the others around here you need to watch out for."

"Okay." It was dawning on Manny that the firm was a place where he could potentially get hurt.

Conference Room B was best used for short morning meetings. The hum of the heating vent and the softness of the leather chairs made for a comforting space that had occasionally seduced some of the most alpha go-getters into snoozing after a heavy lunch.

Jack's meeting was decidedly short and pre-lunch. It was 10:28 a.m. and the nine associates of the Blue Pod were immersed in small talk around the conference table. Jack and Manny entered the room and walked to the head of the table. Silence fell. Jack combed his fingers through his black hair.

"Good morning, children," he said, smiling. "We have a new teacher today. His name is Manny Johnson." Jack often tried to be the slightly witty guy. He liked being characterized as the professional who exceeded the dull personality implied by his résumé. Nevertheless, most pod members still believed the résumé's suggestion was closer to the truth.

"Manny has a solid background in strategy consulting as well as in the telecom and financial industries. He spent some of his early days in the Marines as well. He hails from Kansas City, where he's most recently worked as a consultant for his own boutique strategy outfit." Jack looked around the room to each face as he spoke and made good eye contact. He knew how to present well. "Manny also had the good fortune of going to B-School with me at Columbia." The pod gave a quiet, appropriate ahhh. "Manny, welcome to the Blue Pod."

Manny was blushing a little as the applause subsided. "Thanks. I've been anticipating this time with you. You're a brilliant group of people with exceptional skills. Jack's told me all about your victories. He's also told me about the challenges ahead of us."

He looked around the room. The associates appeared to be listening intently. He continued, "I'm no dummy. I know the best thing I can do as a manager is to get out of the way of your success. I plan to make it easier for you to do what you're already doing. I hope you'll come to see me as the guy who removes the obstacles that hinder your momentum. I'm also looking forward to having some real conversations and getting to know you all. If

you'd like to talk, please stop by my office this week. My door is always open. Thanks."

The group clapped again and Manny took a seat on the side. Jack then introduced the associates around the table and shared brief stories of how each one had saved the day on some project or another. The fifth name he called belonged to a woman with olive skin and wavy black hair. "And this is Linda Flores." She had worked in investment banking on Wall Street before going to both business and law schools. After her studies, Linda practiced as a corporate attorney at an international law firm for three years. She then transitioned to a Latin American telecommunications company, negotiating strategic acquisitions for them in Argentina, Uruguay and Chile.

With her strong background, it was clear that she was the type of professional who kept her eyes on the ball. But for now, she was keeping her eyes on the floor and smiling demurely a Jack waxed on about her achievements. She had contribut more than a few all-night work sessions lately that had hel the pod meet impossible deadlines. "Linda, we couldn't done it without you," Jack concluded. More applause. nodded gratefully. She looked back at Jack, then turned he to Manny.

That was the first time Manny noticed Linda's uncann to make him feel guilty even though he was completely He was occupying the position she had wanted f He couldn't help but wonder what was going on insid

Next, Jack outlined the pod's work to be done in ing week. Their client was the Joval Financial Gr bank in Boston seeking to increase its internationa' Some discouraging economic data had just beer the GDPs of several of the bank's target countri ed on the data's likely effects on the markets. ' and did his best to wash the guilty feeling fro

Linda was sitting across the table. She leaned over to Adam Jacobs, a fellow associate with sandy brown hair and a light beard. He was rubbing it as he leaned in to meet her. Glancing in Manny's direction Linda whispered, "I don't trust him."

CHAPTER THREE

Cyrus & Hopkins was good and bad. At least that's how Susan got the story after Manny's first week at the firm. The work was challenging and high profile—this was good. Manny liked being with Jack and the associates and he was grateful for the firm's Thursday afternoon reception in his honor.

At the same time, things were bad. There were more and more aspects of firm life that really bothered Manny. He noticed that the consultants tended to operate in political silos and avoided collaborating with each other. This was interesting, considering how much the firm bragged to clients about how its pod structure ensured that true teamwork happened. Manny also sensed an undercurrent of arrogance in many of the comments he overheard in meetings. He disliked that. He also started to hear the associates complain that they seldom received clearly defined expectations for success or specific feedback about their work.

One associate, Alex Farber, quit at the end of Manny's first week. So the Blue Pod's nine associates shrank to eight. This consulting firm that was supposed to be fixing other companies' dysfunctions had a boatload of its own. The irony was not lost on Manny.

Finally, there was the ever polite and enigmatic Linda Flores. Manny still had no idea how to read her. Was she about to sabotage him? Was she talking behind his back? Did she respect him at all?

Susan encouraged Manny to give Linda the benefit of the doubt. "After all, why wouldn't you treat her as a friend until proven otherwise?"

On the Tuesday of his second week at the firm, Manny noticed a rift in the pod while he was facilitating a pod meeting. He could tell that it had existed from long ago and was resurfacing.

Some of the associates in the group, like Tom Walker, were relying heavily on quantitative methods of analysis. "The research will point us to the right course of action," he argued at one point.

Other associates, like Adam Jacobs, were relying more on their industry expertise to guide them. "If our recommendation to Joval isn't based on a true understanding of the markets, it's not gonna fly." To Manny, it was clear that both sides had merit; he felt the optimal approach would be a blending of the best from both sides.

The associates felt no need to sugarcoat their exchanges during the meeting. Ideas flew freely but so did the veiled insults ("Only an idiot would think that..."). Manny had encouraged everyone to speak freely, but he also wanted them to speak responsibly. At one point during a volley of quarrelling, he tapped his fingers on the table and cleared his throat. The raised voices continued. He tapped his fingers on the conference table again. Someone yelled, "Guys!" and heads turned toward Manny at the head of the table.

Manny spoke softly. "Long after the current assignment is gone and forgotten, we'll be right here working with each other, so listen carefully." He spoke slowly to reveal intention behind his words. "Don't open your mouth until you've learned how to disagree honorably."

People looked at each other but were initially reluctant to speak. The conversation resumed when Adam volunteered a comment about the psychology behind market behavior. The debate was calm at first, but then grew in intensity until, ten minutes later, voices were raised again and tensions flared. Manny had a headache. At least the insults had stopped; the civil war was slightly more civil. Was it time to go home yet?

After the meeting, Manny headed straight to Jack's office. Jack had seldom been present for meetings that week since somebody had to wine and dine potential new clients. Manny walked though the door. Jack was on the phone and raised his hand to halt Manny from talking. Manny took a seat and waited. Jack was apparently speaking to a transportation and logistics company executive, making plans for lunch. Manny's head was throbbing.

Several minutes passed. Manny stood up to leave but Jack motioned for him to sit down again. He did with a sigh. Why was Jack taking so long? This was irritating.

"So, what can I do for you?" Jack asked while hanging up the phone and picking up his Blackberry.

"There's a rift in the pod between the number crunchers and the industry people. How long has this been going on?"

"Oh, forever. I didn't mention it before because it's easy enough to handle." He spoke while replying to a text message.

"How do you handle them?"

"I choose a side and move on."

"I see."

Jack looked up once his text had flown into cyberspace. "Don't worry about those guys. You have good judgment. Just pick a side and move on." Jack got up from his chair and plucked some files from the cabinet. "I'm going to Seattle tomorrow to meet the guy I was on the phone with. He might be open to retaining us. Keep the pod working on Joval and let me see the draft of the client presentation on Friday when I come back."

"Crap," Manny said under his breath.

The pod's dysfunction and Jack's indifference had put Manny in a sour mood. It was the end of the workday, and he was more than ready to leave the office. Things were not working out as he had planned.

With the passage of ten minutes and a few city blocks, he had finally put some distance between himself and the firm. It was harder, though, to leave his cares behind. A cloud of disillusionment followed Manny as he wove in and out of people on the busy sidewalk. In his thoughts, he was kicking himself: I should have done more due diligence. I should have noticed this life-sucking, oppressive corporate culture before I took the job. What did I set myself up for?

He raced down the subway steps two at a time, overtaking a man in an olive suit who was walking too slowly. He swiped his Metro Card and flew through the turnstile, wondering how the Blue Pod could be so messed up. What could he possibly do to turn around such a well-entrenched dynamic? Was *this* what he and his family had moved to New York for? He quickly pushed that thought out of his mind—too depressing to consider. He reached the train platform and found himself mentioning to no one in particular, "I don't know if I can do this." The woman standing next to him smiled and took a step away.

The ride took about forty minutes. He had to change from the 1 train to the 7 train at Times Square. While traveling through the tunnel under the East River, Manny distracted himself by reading the latest subway advertisements overhead. There was an ad for a dermatologist with remarkable "before" and "after" pictures of a woman's acne-ridden face. Another ad promoted a language school that taught English to immigrants and helped them obtain student visas to stay in the U.S.

Manny got off the train at the 41st Street stop in Sunnyside. He walked along Queens Boulevard and turned left by the White

Castle restaurant on 43rd Street. Within a few minutes, he arrived at the red brick house he had recently learned to call his home.

He spent his usual time with Ryan and Samantha, asking them about their day at school and playing with them. He then went into the kitchen and helped Susan prepare dinner. He told her about the dysfunctions of the pod while he chopped carrots. At one point, he stopped chopping and leaned against the counter. "Honey, I don't know if I can turn this thing around."

Susan had oven mitts on and was pulling a pan of lasagna from the top rack of the oven. "Give it some more time. It's still early." She carefully brought the pan into the dining room and placed it on top of a potholder on the table. "You really can't know what's possible with the group until you get your bearings."

Manny nodded and called the children in from the front room. He helped get them seated and circled around the table, kissing everyone on their foreheads. "Love you guys. See you later." Then he walked to the front closet and grabbed his coat. He wouldn't be eating at home that night since he had made plans for dinner with his old friend Noah.

Manny passed through the door of the Thai restaurant and immediately spotted Noah amidst the bustle of the crowd. Manny was reminded of how much Noah resembled his father. The red hair, the brown eyes, the smile. Noah was wearing a long, navy blue coat and had a leather briefcase in hand. He was no longer the scraggly little kid that Manny had befriended in the desert.

The friends embraced and sat at the bar since there was a wait for the table. The bartender filled two frosty glasses with beer. "Thanks again for helping us unpack last weekend," Manny said.

"No problemo. I'll find a way for you to pay me back."

Manny chuckled, "What are you talking about? Your slave labor is one of the main reasons we moved to New York. Speaking of which, you're still watching the kids for us on Saturday night, right?"

Noah smiled. "Don't worry. I gotcha. Saturday."

Manny looked at the flattened mess of red hair on Noah's head. He then identified the offending item on the countertop: a baseball cap that Noah had been wearing a minute ago. "You have an acute case of hat-head."

Noah raised his hands, felt his head and confirmed his status. He manipulated his hair halfway to decency then shrugged his shoulders. "Whatever."

The concerns of the workday were still knocking around in the back of Manny's mind. He tried to keep them way back, to keep them from showing up on his face. He just wanted to enjoy himself now. But you can't hide the truth from the eyes of a discerning friend. "You look like hell," Noah remarked.

Manny raised his glass. Shaking his head, he said, "Here's to honesty."

"Talk to me, buddy."

There was a pause as Manny gathered his thoughts. He was grateful for Noah's ear. Noah and Susan were the two people in the world he could trust with his unfiltered thoughts, so he unloaded. "This job is not what I was looking for. The guys in the office don't seem to be on my wavelength."

"You mean they care about different things than you do?"

"Yeah. Exactly. I mean they talk like they're concerned about the firm's problems, but then they behave like they don't care." Manny described the dilemmas *du jour*: the sarcasm, the cynicism and the isolationism. The sucky employee retention, the office political issues that people tiptoed around, the lack of collaboration, and the arrogance. And of course, the rift in the pod and the fact that pod members weren't listening to each other. "I could handle it all a lot better if Jack would support me more, but he's always off doing something else. Who knows? Maybe it's better this way since his leadership style is so different from mine. It's going to be a little weird when we actually co-lead the group."

Noah listened quietly for about ten minutes, shifting from time to time on his uncomfortable bar stool. He finally offered, "Man, I'm sorry that you're hurting like this. I know how it feels to be majorly disappointed."

"Thanks." Manny took a sip. "I've given up a lot to come to Cyrus & Hopkins. But I didn't come here so I could play Mr. Heavy with the pod. Honestly, it feels like I've joined the crew of a ship that's sinking out at sea. The question is whether we can bail water fast enough to repair it."

With all the clamor and Muzak in the background, the men didn't hear the hostess yell, "Johnson, party of two." She had to repeat the call before they got up and grabbed their coats.

As they navigated toward the hostess's desk, Manny dropped the bomb, "I hate to say it, but if this keeps up, I may have to start considering some other options."

The hostess walked them to a table by the window and left them with their huge menus. Manny sat down, feeling good about getting everything off his chest. "I'm glad you're working just a few blocks away from me. I have a feeling you're gonna be my link to sanity in the coming weeks."

Noah returned, "You've been there for me too, more times than I can remember." He picked up his menu and examined it. "I wonder what the specials are today."

There was something in Noah's tone. Just a hint of preoccupation. Manny knew the voice. Some significant piece of advice was being crafted and Noah was contemplating how to phrase it. Manny was enjoying reading Noah's mind; at last he was on somebody's wavelength.

"So," Manny pondered aloud, "are you going to keep all the good stuff to yourself? Let me hear your thoughts."

Noah looked up from behind his extraordinary menu. He knew better than to try hiding the truth. "Let me order my food first and I'll tell you what I'm thinking."

He kept his word once they had ordered. "You need to remember who you are."

Manny raised his eyebrows and lowered them again. "I'm listening."

"I care about your shutting down your personality more than I care about your dysfunctional office. The firm is obviously messed up, but remember..." He looked around conspiratorially. "There's a revolutionary inside you. The ship may be sinking, but you've got what it takes to either repair the ship or at least go down fighting! You've gotta be yourself no matter the cost. Remember Mexico?"

One of the perks Manny had with his own business back in Kansas City was that he could take month-long vacations with his family every summer. Noah, who was godfather to both Johnson kids, had vacationed with the family each year for the past three years. Their last adventure centered around a beach house in Los Cabos, Mexico.

"The Manny I knew in Mexico was a carefree and natural leader. When you're around your family and me, you're not afraid to be yourself—the most authentic you—all the time. Whenever problems came up in Los Cabos, part of the solution included you laughing, loving and enjoying life! But you're holding back now that you're at Cyrus & Hopkins with their 'serious' culture. I've known you forever. You probably could come up with a dozen great ideas about how to fix your dysfunctional pod. I know you'd have a real impact too, but you've got to build up the courage to act on what you know. You need to get over your split personality."

Manny started to remember the conversations about split personalities he'd had with Susan and Noah on their terrace overlooking el Océano Pacífico. He remembered Susan describing the unspoken office rule that plagued too much of Corporate America: don't be your real self *too much* around the office. You're not allowed to show that you care about a co-worker beyond the minimum required for social niceties. Don't even think about having a discussion with your colleague about the struggles you're having with your kids at home. Play it safe at work.

He recalled Noah protesting how everyone seemed to live by the CYA rule at work. You're not allowed to admit that you made a mistake. You're not allowed to have an "off" day every now and then. You don't get to talk about your life's dreams. You should definitely not expect anyone to care about developing you professionally—at least don't expect them to care beyond the minimum needed to keep you quiet. And why do we have to pretend that our knowledge about life and love doesn't apply to leading people at work? Does our life's wisdom become magically invalid as soon as we step foot into an office building?

Everybody agreed while watching those Mexican sunsets over the ocean that there were two sets of rules most people lived by: one set for home life and an inferior version for work. Don't you dare mix the two so you can have a whole life. Your boss expects you to have a split personality disorder like everyone else around here.

Noah's appetizer arrived. He continued, "Split personalities are so overrated. Very unhealthy. You and Susan are such good leaders with the kids. Why can't you bring the person you are at home to work? I mean do it full volume. Turn the volume up on who you are at work." He took a bite of his skewered chicken satay and widened his eyes to signal great pleasure. "You know you want to."

Manny nodded.

Noah squinted his eyes. He used an I-know-what-you're-up-to voice. "You're holding back. Your associates aren't getting the

full Manny like your friends and family do. How can you write
your pod off as hopeless when you haven't given them all you've
got? That's not you. You never leave a challenge without giving it
your best."

Manny was staring at his plate. He was daydreaming about
how easy everything was back in his old consulting shop.
But things were different now. Now he was subject to Jack's
authority and no one else in the pod seemed to be living for what
Manny was living for.

Noah took another bite and said while chewing, "Guuuuud."
He looked up to make sure Manny was okay and then decided to
continue. "Forget the firm's culture. Your associates are tired of
performing in a culture of fakeness and pretending. What they
need is your help. They're looking for real life in a barren place.
Just like we did back in the desert. I know you can make that
happen for them."

Manny was weighing what good could possibly come from
sacrificing himself for some invisible sense that things could be
better. He was battling real fear as he considered the prospect of
nakedly living out his values in a place where his colleagues
didn't share them. But fear wasn't the only thing he felt. Other
dynamics were blending in too. Something in his heart was
responding to the idea of living an authentic life, no matter the
cost. He liked the idea of being the kind of man who committed
to that. Perhaps there was a little more fight left in Manny after
all. Or perhaps not. "But Noah, it's not easy being the only one
who gives a damn. This could be a losing battle and it's my butt
on the line."

Noah shrugged his shoulders. "So what if you lose? Really.
All that matters is that you act honorably to the end. That's all
that you control—your actions. And we both know that some of
your honor is going to rub off on the people in your pod. Don't
pretend you can't help them grow. You have a powerful track
record in developing teams."

It was true. Manny had always loved helping people become whom they were meant to be, even when it was a challenging task. That's why he'd used his free time in Kansas City to coach Ryan's Little League games. He'd volunteered to fulfill various mentoring roles over the years. The challenge of developing the Blue Pod associates was appealing to Manny.

Noah looked him right in the eyes. "I know you. You can do this. I dare you to make it happen."

Manny had been on the receiving end of Noah's and Susan's encouragement before. They'd all encouraged each other many times, even on this issue. Yet something was different this time. Something had shifted. The weight of countless years of encouragement had moved an internal boundary in Manny's heart. Somehow, Manny no longer believed that the pod's problems were bigger than him.

Manny surprised himself and said, "Challenge accepted."

Within seconds, the chinking of beer mugs was heard and they drank. They used a toast that Noah had learned in the Marines, "L'chaim! To life!" Manny took a long draw from his beer and proclaimed, "This is going to be epic!"

❖   ❖   ❖

CHAPTER FOUR

The next morning, Manny strode down the firm's corridor like he knew his place in the world. He entered his office and closed the door. He dropped his briefcase on his desk and jumped onto the couch, landing horizontally and bouncing twice. He clasped his hands behind his head. Joy had taken root in his heart and he felt like starting the day by dreaming about how he could adapt lessons from his life and bring them to work. He'd always believed that there was a way to be professional and personal in any environment. Now was his chance to invent this equilibrium in a new context.

He grabbed a pad from the coffee table and scribbled down things he'd learned from his family, Noah, his military squad and everywhere else. His thoughts ran briefly to his older brother Caleb, who had inspired his passion for life when Manny was just a boy.

Manny was pleasantly surprised as he realized that the pod's dysfunctions weren't bothering him anymore. He began to understand that his job wasn't to fix everything. His job was to do his best and let the chips fall where they may. He knew he could do that, now that his mind was made up.

A question surfaced: what if the partners, the powers that be, reject me?

He thought about it and instantly chose his response: Oh well. If I perish, I perish. I'll go down fighting. And at least I get to be me.

He thought about how so many people hang their hearts up at the front door of their office buildings every morning. They live a disconnected existence at work and call it professionalism. They only get to collect their heart again at the end of the day when they head out the office doors. The process is repeated daily until one day, they head for the doors but their hearts are missing. Thoughts run through their heads: What were my priorities before office politics consumed me? I've forgotten who I am. Didn't I want to change the world? What ever happened to my playful personality? What's so great about the work I'm doing here? What are my dreams again?

Manny took pleasure in knowing that his associates would never have to work in such a dismal world as long as he was leading them.

The first challenge to Manny's exuberance came in the form of that morning's pod meeting in Conference Room B. The associates had cleaned up their language, but they still were at a standstill over the direction the client presentation should take. Despite Manny's entreaties for the pod to arrive at a consensus, the two factions remained polarized. Manny felt the urge to override the pod's bickering and make the decision himself. "Pick a side and move on," Jack had said. However, Manny wanted more than a quick solution; he wanted the pod to become a true team. So he resisted pulling rank and tried to come up with a creative plan to guide the pod into effectiveness. He settled on an idea he'd used before on his kids at home.

He got up and went to the back corner of the room where there was a table with a pitcher of water and glasses. "Who'd like some water?" he asked over his shoulder as he poured a glass. No one answered. Was this a trick question? No one was comfortable with the idea of managers serving beverages to associates. No one wanted to be the first to test the waters. He poured another glass and turned around with the two. "You know, doctors say you should have eight glasses a day." A few people chuckled politely. "No one's thirsty?"

"I'm thirsty," said Linda. "I'll take a glass." Manny walked over and placed a glass in her hands. "Thanks," she said with an interesting smile.

Manny wasn't sure whether it was a condescending smile or not. He felt a twinge of that guilt he tended to feel around Linda. He decided to let the matter go. He couldn't control Linda but he could control himself. "You're welcome. Any other takers?" Two more associates spoke up so he gave the remaining glass in his hand, went back to the table, filled another glass and served it.

Standing at the head of the table, he announced, "There are two sides to this argument. We've heard from each one at length. I now want each side to present the merits of the *other* side's case for five minutes. Who wants to go first?" He was greeted by a throng of dumbfounded faces. No one volunteered so Manny selected the three most vocal proponents on each side. When they finally spoke, he made sure they argued passionately. "More emotion! Louder!" The pod was in a state of shock. The associates looked at him with blank expressions. "Trust me," was his only response.

After the industry side presented the case they'd heard from the number crunchers, Manny asked the crunchers to rate how well the industry folks had listened to them (they gave a four out of ten). Then it was the number crunchers' turn to argue the industry case (a three out of ten).

As if that weren't strange enough, Manny then declared, "No one's leaving the room until both teams have achieved a score of at least eight. So find out what you need to do to improve your score. And yes, you can leave to pee if you need to." The reactions on the pod's faces ranged from amazement to disgust. This was definitely not the way Jack used to do things.

The presentations lasted all morning and halfway through lunch. Finally, both teams listened well enough to achieve an eight. After lunch break, the meeting's discussion took on a very different tenor. <u>The consultants had learned to empathize with each other and a subtle shift happened in their exchanges. Instead of using their words to win the argument at hand, people started using their words to uncover the best solution</u>. They didn't reach a consensus, but they came close.

Linda sat silently in her leather chair through most of the meeting. Manny chose not to press her to speak. She eventually offered a few words in the late afternoon, but nothing of consequence.

At the end of the day, Adam and Linda walked together out of the room and down the hallway. Adam commented, "You know how Jack is always saying, 'Our people are our most important asset?'"

"Yeah," Linda replied. "I don't really get the impression that he means it much."

"I know. I hate that. But Manny seems different. Don't you think?"

Linda searched Adam's face for signs of sarcasm. Finding none, she said, "He did well today." Why disclose what's best left unsaid? she thought. He's not for real. He has some moves and he's everyone's darling today, but it won't last. It's probably some well-rehearsed shtick of his. Give him some time. He'll turn out to be like every other power-seeking opportunist around here. "We'll see how things go," Linda added. She was well acquainted with the ache of hoping for too much, yet she couldn't deny that she still longed for much more from her career.

On Thursday, Manny started the pod meeting by saying, "Today is the day we'll achieve a consensus on the strategy we'll propose to Joval." The pod needed a common framework for the varied research findings and recommendations that each associate had produced over the prior weeks, according to their individual areas of expertise. The client meeting would be on

Monday at Joval's Boston headquarters. Each pod member had to arrange his or her individual thoughts for inclusion in the group's power presentation slides that Jack and Manny would present. Hopefully, the slides would equip the bank's executives with the information they needed to pursue a bold new overseas expansion strategy—a different strategy than what the bank had considered thus far.

Before diving into debate, Manny had each associate share his or her findings. Each associate was already roughly aware of the others' recommendations, but as the details of the research process were shared, they began to grasp the nuances behind the recommendations. Manny would chime in from time to time to remind everyone of how the details related to the big picture. The discussion lasted for the better part of the morning.

The next step was to weave the different components into a seamless and logical flow of ideas; they needed a consensus on a framework. At this point, Manny strolled to the side of the room and picked up a brown cardboard box off the floor. He came back to the center of the room and turned the box upside down, releasing a flurry of multi-colored koosh balls on the table. "Everybody grab some."

Linda looked incredulously as each consultant returned to their seat with a stash of the soft toys. Yesterday's little exercise was cute, but was Manny going to turn everyday into pre-school? Would they get milk and cookies before naptime?

"I know you're wondering if we're going to be doing crazy things all the time. The answer is I don't know. Probably not all the time. But maybe. It all depends on what you show me you need. I'm willing to do whatever it takes for you guys to learn how to be a real team."

"But we are a team." Linda had spoken. The associates looked around at each other. "We've had our problems, but we've been a team, long before you came."

Manny was glad to hear something other than honeyed super-ficialities from Linda's mouth. He smiled at her. "This pod has called itself a team for a while, but actually you've been acting more like a workgroup." He paced around the table as he spoke. "You're all used to doing your work separately and then coming together, but you're not used to depending on each other for your results. You never learned how to gel as a team. Today is impor-tant because we're learning how to collaborate and depend on each other in a high stakes situation. We need results and we'll win or lose together."

Linda was staring at the papers in front of her. Manny contin-ued, "But your point is taken, Linda. You have friendships with each other. You've helped each other in some ways. But what I'm saying is that you've not yet learned how to produce results as a team. And, as we all know, results are mandatory."

Linda nodded to accept the point.

So Manny initiated the strategy formulation by making every-one brainstorm together. "The rules are simple. No one is wrong while we're brainstorming. Speak freely without fear of failure. Ideas that are far out there are great because some facet of your idea may be just what we need to inspire a solution. If anyone starts to edit or criticize an idea prematurely, everyone has to throw koosh balls at him." This is going to be fun, he thought.

Manny stood next to the whiteboard and transcribed the ideas as the brainstorming began. One idea, two ideas, then three. Lee Evers offered a fourth idea. He was a tall, African-American fellow whom most of the firm's women found highly attractive. Adam, however, found Lee's latest idea less than attractive. Adam only caught himself halfway through describing how Lee's strate-gy could alienate the bank's investors. He remembered too late. Koosh balls flew from every direction. Adam was pummeled and the table erupted in laughter. The faucet had been opened. They laughed for a much longer time than Manny expected. Even Adam had to laugh.

As the brainstorming resumed, Tom Walker, the pod's blond, blue-eyed maverick, encountered death by koosh ball too. So did Lee Evers. They all survived with everything but their pride intact. The beginning of a shift had occurred. The tenor of the pod's verbal exchanges was light-years away from Tuesday's shouting contest. A weight had been lifted. The pod no longer took itself so seriously.

Then the miraculous happened. The associates looked at each other in disbelief when a particularly brilliant suggestion was aired. Could they have stumbled onto the killer framework they so needed? Indeed they had, and they knew it. Manny glanced at his watch and noticed that they had been brainstorming for thirty-five minutes when they struck gold.

And it was Linda who bestowed the golden words that galvanized the team into consensus. She was the source of the middle-of-the-road plan that was right on point. The approach integrated the best of both the worlds: it pleased the number crunchers and it satisfied the industry wonks.

The whole pod broke out in applause. It was a different type of applause than was heard before. It was heartfelt. Manny erupted too, "Good work! Let's all go to lunch together! I'm buying and Linda gets the seat of honor!" The applause ratcheted up to a new level of merriment.

Louise the receptionist sauntered down the hallway past the glass conference room door, trying to look casual. She was investigating the source of the commotion. Such sounds were not usually heard in the corridors of Cyrus & Hopkins.

After the victory lunch, Manny stopped off at his office to return email and voicemail messages. He finished his calls and got up from his desk to rejoin the pod in the conference room. When he rose, he realized he forgot something, so he plopped down in the chair again. He picked up the phone and dialed. There was a voicemail greeting on the other end. He waited for the beep and spoke. "Hey, Noah, it's Manny. It's working. The pod's turning around. You dared me, and I did it. Thanks, pal."

That afternoon Manny asked Linda to write a one-page document outlining her approach. The pod used the document to guide them as they assembled their work into the presentation slides on a laptop in the conference room. By 4:30 they had a decent-looking draft ready to show Jack early the next morning.

More brainstorming followed. Manny rehearsed the presentation out loud. When he finished, everyone tried to guess the questions that were likely to arise from the bank executives. What would our answers be? What were the weaknesses of the case we were making? This was a big deal. This client presentation was ultimately what the bank was paying for. The pod wanted to make their partner, Jack, look good. Increasingly, they also wanted to make their manager Manny look good when he co-presented with Jack.

No one was more surprised than Linda when she found herself offering ideas at every turn that afternoon. Everyone knew her to be a reserved contributor. Her style was to remain quiet until she perceived just the right time to outshine all with a powerful insight. But now Linda was dispensing suggestions at every turn. And even more disturbing to her, she could have even sworn she felt a slight desire to see Manny succeed in Boston.

Her thoughts were interrupted by Manny's voice. "Linda and Adam, I want you to come to Boston. You both know every detail of this project, and unlike me, you've been on the assignment from the start. You'll be good backup for us when we get client questions." It was the firm's custom to limit the number of associates who accompanied partners and managers for the client presentation. Travel costs were a concern, but also too many consultants could make the client executives feel outnumbered.

Manny felt his mobile phone vibrating in pocket. It was Jack. Manny excused himself and brought the phone into the hallway. "Hey. What's up?"

When Manny walked back into the room, his face was not a happy one. "Guys, Jack's catching the red-eye back from Seattle so we'll go through the presentation in the morning as planned. He also mentioned that he got a call from the EVP of International Operations at Joval. Basically, we have a problem."

The specifics were these: Lee and Adam had generated their conclusions based on data from the internal reports supplied by the Joval Financial Group. In talking with the executive vice president, Jack discovered that part of the data in the internal reports was based on incorrect assumptions. Therefore, Lee and Adam's conclusions were invalid. The newly corrected internal reports had already been sent by hand courier to the firm's offices and would arrive within ten minutes, by 7 p.m.

Manny continued, "Rest assured, the integrity of our overall approach is not in question. Only one section's data needs to be tweaked. And I don't think Lee and Adam's recommendations for that section will have to be adjusted too much." Manny sorted his papers and effects and pocketed them in his leather case. "Jack wants us to go over the revised presentation at 9:45 a.m. tomorrow, so it looks like I have some number crunching to do. I should be able to knock it out tonight barring any unforeseen problems. I'll see you all in the morning."

The associates packed up their items and tossed their koosh balls back into the box, which now had a home on the side of the room.

"Lee and Adam, could I speak with you?" asked Manny. They approached with concern on their faces. "Guys, don't worry about this. Obviously this is not your fault. I'll work on the reports and see how the revised figures affect things. Come by my office at six thirty tomorrow morning. I'll show you how I think the new numbers should modify our recommendations. If you disagree with me and I think you have merit, we can incorporate your new ideas into the presentation before the meeting with Jack." Manny grinned. "That's assuming either of you would be foolish enough to disagree with me." They laughed.

Reality sunk in as Manny made his way back to his office. He might only get an hour or two of sleep that night. There was too much work to be done. He also was dreading the phone call he had to make. "Sorry guys. Daddy has to work late tonight. What was the best thing that happened to you in school today? What was the worst? Don't give Mommy a hard time when she says it's time to go to bed. I love you."

It was 11:11 p.m. Manny got up from his desk once he realized that his bleary eyes had covered the same page three times without comprehending any of it. His eyelids were heavy. He walked around his office. He paused by the window. A moonless night made for a dark sky. He noted how the shadowed expanse of Central Park was framed by the brilliance of the city lights surrounding it. His mind randomly jumped to a memory of his backyard in Kansas City. How he missed pushing Samantha and Ryan on the swings there. The garden he had cultivated over the years. He knew each square inch of it—the small grapevine, the tomatoes.

At 11:23 p.m., his cell phone buzzed. "Jack Jameson" flashed on its colorful screen.

"Manny, you got the reports?"

"No worries, I'm working on them now. We'll be fine by the morning."

"Good. By the way, I just found out that Deborah Hopkins will be joining us for the Joval presentation on Monday."

Manny swiveled in his chair. "Wow. Is that typical—for the managing partner to come for a client presentation?"

"No. It's just that she's a personal friend of the EVP who retained us."

Manny wasn't sure how he felt about this development.

Jack interrupted his introspection. "This is your big chance to let Deborah see what you can do. Get ready to dazzle. Alright, I'll catch you in the morning."

"Wait, before you go, I wanted to run something by you." Manny stood up as if to shake off any hint of his sleepiness. Or perhaps he rose to feel less small, the way you do when making a request you know is a stretch. "I have an idea about Linda..." He made a proposal. Jack said he would think about it. They ended the conversation and Manny went back to the document he was reading before.

At 11:41 p.m., Manny's face was illumined by the grayish light of the spreadsheet on his monitor. He was inputting the numbers into a model but had to stop. He was feeling sore from sitting in his chair too long. He arched his back and stretched his arms. He was looking back down at the computer screen a moment later when he felt someone's presence near. He looked up to find Adam and Lee walking through his doorway. They drifted over to the discussion area and settled into the couch and chair.

Manny's heart rose. "Hi. What are you guys doing here?"

Lee replied, "Those revisions can take longer than you'd think. Need any help?"

Manny was too tired to try to hide his bliss. He thanked them profusely and brought the reports over to the coffee table where Adam was now setting up his laptop. The three of them attacked the numbers together. They worked, made jokes, got coffee, worked some more and ended up going home around 2 a.m.

When Manny crawled under his comforter and nuzzled into Susan's side that night, he noticed himself smiling. True, he was appreciating the smell of Susan's hair and the precious sleep he would be afforded, but his smile had another cause as well. It was now official: Manny had detected signs of life in the barren landscape of Cyrus & Hopkins.

PART TWO

❖   ❖   ❖

The Surprise

CHAPTER FIVE

There's no better way to ruin a silk tie than to sneeze while drinking coffee. Jack was walking on a busy sidewalk when it happened. The blue skies over Boston did little to comfort him about the dark stain on his yellow tie. Good thing he had packed an extra one. He rounded the street corner and went inside the Joval Financial Building in the Back Bay area. He made a beeline to an office for visiting consultants on the twelfth floor.

Once there, he greeted Manny, Linda and Adam and yanked a new red tie from his briefcase. He lifted his collar and started looping the tie around it. He used his reflection in a window to guide himself. His mobile phone rang halfway through his Windsor knot. Deborah Hopkins. She was calling from a taxi to confirm that she had just landed at Logan.

Jack checked his watch to find a mere hour and twenty minutes between him and the meeting's start time. The consultants were buzzing around the room in last-minute activity. He warned them of the time and rounded it off with a "Let's go" aimed at Adam. Adam followed him upstairs, carrying a large box filled with documents to accompany the presentation. The two of them were off to prepare the boardroom and double-check the audiovisual equipment. Linda and Manny remained.

"Let's walk through the presentation deck one more time," Manny said, his hair still somewhat darkened with dampness from his shower earlier that morning. "And as we go through it this time, I have a surprise for you."

"A surprise?"

Manny swept his arm in the direction of a chair and said, "Yes, a surprise."

Linda obliged and sat down, reflecting on how much she hated surprises an hour and twenty minutes before show time. Yet, Manny was halfway smirking. This had better be good.

Manny sat down on top of the desk next to her. "Jack and I have decided that you should give the presentation. You know the project details inside out. You know the presentation by heart. The strategy was originally your idea. It's right for you to present it."

"Umm, thanks, but no," she said quickly. "It's better for you and Jack to present. Deborah Hopkins will be there." Most other associates would have gracefully turned him down too, being frightened at the prospect of speaking publicly without much notice. But not Linda. Her thoughts were elsewhere: Somebody pinch me. After years of sacrificing without the barest hint of recognition, is someone finally acknowledging me? Manny is a discerning guy. Surely he can tell that when I said no, I didn't actually mean to decline. Or was I too curt for him to perceive that challenge was a false one?

Manny took in her eyes, scratched his chin and got up. He strode a few paces toward the door. He turned again and faced her direction. "Would it make any difference to know that I want you to present?"

And so the truth was enticed out of the shadows. There was no suppressing it. Linda smiled. It was the kind of grin that called on the stars of the universe for its brightness.

She thanked Manny for the chance and, for a split second, she questioned whether she was prepared enough to lead the show.

The moment soon passed, however, as she realized what Manny already knew: that she'd had the presentation memorized since Friday when she led Manny and Jack through its ins and outs. She was ready.

The client presentation started on time in the Joval boardroom. The room was full with the senior leadership of the bank. Deborah sat with her fellow consultants. As anticipated, the proposed business strategy recommended a different direction than the executives were expecting. There were more than a few raised eyebrows, however, the apprehension on their faces dissipated a little more with every slide. Linda facilitated the meeting flawlessly and with confidence. By Manny's estimate, most of the decision-makers had come onboard by the second section of slides. By the end of the entire presentation, everyone could tell that the Joval Financial Group would adopt the new strategy.

Jack, Manny and Adam made their contributions during the Q&A time. It stretched into a considerable discussion. Deborah Hopkins was pleased when she saw the clients' reactions. She didn't know what to make of Manny and Jack's decision to let Linda have the spotlight, but she wasn't about to argue with success. Deborah made her way over to Linda and congratulated her immediately after the Q&A. "Manny told me the strategy was your idea." Linda didn't know what to say except, "thanks." It was the third time that she'd ever gotten to speak with Deborah. It was also the first time that a boss had ever cited Linda's individual contributions to the managing partner.

Jack was strangely anxious throughout the meeting. He had grudgingly agreed to let Linda lead only because Manny had insisted so strongly. While sitting through the slides, he found it curious that a part of him wanted Linda to falter, just a bit.

The meeting adjourned and the crowd spread out over the boardroom, mingling in clusters of polite conversation. There was a palpable optimism about the bank's future overseas.

The Joval executives eventually cleared out, taking Deborah with them. Jack finally walked over to Linda and Adam with his hand extended. "Good job today."

After debriefing with them, he noticed Manny packing up some items across the room. It was time for Jack to put the finishing touch on the victorious day by congratulating Manny. He started to walk in Manny's direction, but something stopped him. An irksome knot in his stomach. He altered his course and arrived at the audiovisual control panel instead.

Linda took delight in orchestrating a personal victory celebration in the airline waiting lounge at Boston's Logan Airport. The festivities that afternoon included a forbidden copy of *People* magazine along with a tall, skim, double-shot mocha with whipped cream. She heard the loudspeaker announce the boarding of her shuttle flight to New York. Adam hadn't arrived at the airport yet. Jack had obviously kept him at Joval longer than expected. They'll just have to catch the next flight in an hour, she thought.

She boarded the MD-88 aircraft with her roll-aboard bag in tow. She was destined for seat 23-E, a window seat. That side of the plane had two adjacent seats. Perhaps the seat next to hers would be vacant so she could stretch out in flight. She made her way down the long, narrow aisle and looked up from her boarding pass to find her row number. She lifted her bag into the overhead bin. This was no easy feat to accomplish without spilling her mocha. She glanced down and saw Manny Johnson sitting in the aisle seat next to her window. Surprise.

Noreen at the firm's travel agency sometimes took the initiative to reserve pod members' seats together. Linda wasn't appreciating Noreen's initiative right then. Linda wanted some alone time on the flight to process her changing attitude about Manny.

"Hey there," Manny said. "Are you in the window?"

She gestured toward the seat. "That's me."

Manny stood up and moved aside for Linda to pass through. The two buckled themselves in and waited. Linda mentioned the surprisingly good food she'd discovered at some restaurant on Commonwealth Avenue. Manny discussed how his kids wanted to explore Central Park with him that upcoming weekend. The light conversation lasted until takeoff when Linda turned and watched the city and its bay shrink outside.

Her thoughts turned to what had happened that morning. She didn't understand why Manny had passed up the chance to shine in front of Deborah Hopkins. It made her feel uncomfortable that he had done that. What did he expect in return now? She spoke to the window, "You really didn't need to do what you did... for me."

An unhurried smile crept across Manny's face. A few seconds of silence. "I wanted to."

She pushed against her seatback and reclined. She spread an airline blanket over herself and closed her eyes. "Well, thank you. I'm going to rest."

A few minutes later, the rattling of the beverage cart was heard and the flight attendant stopped by row 23. He offered Manny a drink and some peanuts. Manny turned down the peanuts, but took a ginger ale. The attendant studied Linda, but left her alone since her eyes were closed.

Her eyes were closed, but she was actually far from sleep. Thoughts raced through her mind as she tried to understand what had happened at the client site. Perhaps she'd been too skeptical of her new boss. Perhaps he was a decent guy. She considered the unselfconscious way Manny had always seemed to care for whomever came within his reach. He was so intentional about everything and yet so free. She also reflected on how she and other Blue Pod members now felt freer to be themselves at work. Hurricane Manny had swept in and had changed the rules. How did he do that?

Linda adjusted her blanket to cover her neck. She concluded that Manny was probably doing a better job leading the pod than she would have. Remarkably, her conclusion was not accompanied by jealousy. She smiled. Linda, you're growing up. She was okay with the fact that she still had more to learn about inspiring others.

A few minutes later, the P.A. system announced that it was now safe to move about the cabin. A relentless procession of thoughts continued through Linda's head. How does he do it? He seems to be living what he believes. But what does he believe? He's purposefully gentle, but there's nothing weak about him. He's got strong convictions and he demands results. And he's getting results from us! She opened her eyes, pulled her seatback forward and looked to Manny.

Manny turned to meet her, a quizzical eyebrow raised. Fumbling for words, she voiced, "How do you do it?" She coughed out of nervousness. "You know... you just arrive at the firm, out of the blue, acting like you don't notice that you do things differently than everybody else."

His other brow rose too. His confusion had turned to astonishment.

"It's the way you greet everyone, 'How are you?' and then you wait for a real response. It's the way you pass up presentations in front of Deborah like, 'No problem. No sweat.' It's the way you change workgroups into teams. There's something different about you."

Manny couldn't believe his ears. Was this really *Linda* talking this way? He didn't know what to say. He finished his last sip of ginger ale.

Amazingly, she continued, "And while the other partners and managers are just... just managing people, it feels like you're really leading us somewhere. We're working together and we have a vision." She was taken aback momentarily by how good it felt to be open with him—her boss. "So how do you do it? Do you have to be born a natural leader or can I learn how?"

He stared at the airline insignia on his plastic cup, at a loss for words. He was genuinely touched. Finally, the words came. "Thank you." He looked at her. "I respect your opinion, so what you said means a lot to me. As to your question about leadership, I'll be honest with you." He chuckled under his breath. "I wasn't born a natural leader. I used to be the guy no one paid attention to. I had to learn how to lead. I had to. The way I see things, I've been given a great honor by every organization I've worked for, including Cyrus & Hopkins. I've been entrusted with the power and frailty of human beings to accomplish our mission. All of my direct reports may be consultants, but they're also more than that. They're mothers, husbands, brothers and best friends. They have real dreams. They matter. The way I treat them impacts hundreds of people beyond the walls of our office, so I have to lead skillfully. I owe it to our people." Manny looked straight up, as if searching for words. "I've known the basics of good leading for a while now, but, truthfully, I only found the courage to fully practice what I believe last week."

"You mean you didn't lead the same way before you came to the firm?"

"Yes and no. I led this way before, but my style was a watered-down version of what you've been seeing. What happened last week was that a good friend helped me to turn up the volume on what I already had in my heart."

"So you're still learning how to lead."

He laughed. "Of course. And I'll always be learning. Why would I ever want to stop growing?"

Linda exhaled. She was grateful that she had built up enough courage to start a straightforward conversation. "Forgive me if this sounds less than reverential, but growth doesn't seem to be a high priority for most of the leaders at our firm."

"I hear you. A lot of so-called leaders fail to lead even though they have people reporting to them. I even know some CEOs who are remarkable strategists but who've never been broken in as leaders. They're underdeveloped when it comes to achieving their missions through people. Then they wonder why their corporate strategies never get executed well."

Linda reflected on her own history. "I've had a string of inconsequential bosses who never learned how to achieve results through people. It's disheartening to work for bosses like that."

"You were right to long for more. Something was missing."

Linda settled a little more deeply into her seat. Was she finally talking to someone who understood what it meant to be both effective and human?

Manny continued, "I've served under different leaders in Corporate America and felt that longing too. I used to wonder about what my bosses lacked. And then, when I started to lead my own people, I had to admit that even my own leadership style was lacking what I longed for. For years I couldn't put my finger on what that crazy, missing substance was."

"I have a hunch that you eventually found the missing part."

"The answer is simple, but not easy." Manny smiled. "You have to have a love for life. As crazy as it may sound, the answer is life. Life is the main thing you need to get others to follow your lead. You've got to make life happen, otherwise your leading is useless."

He looked at Linda to find the expression of uncertainty he knew would be there. "Now the question of course is, 'What do I mean by "life" exactly?' Well, when I say life, I mean your optimal state of being. Real life. Not just surviving, but thriving. For example, I don't want our pod members to just go through the motions at work and only have their most basic human needs met. I want you all to experience a sense of purpose and a community that are way bigger than you. I want you to dive into an adventure and make meaningful results happen at work. That's the kind of life a leader's got to make happen for himself and his people. That kind of life is the only context that can sustain a high performance team forever."

"Where did this life idea come from—I mean—how did you become so interested in the concept?"

Manny sighed and sorted through his thoughts. "My family moved to a new neighborhood back when I was in grade school. I think it was the third grade. I got pretty sick shortly after we moved and, as a result, I lost a lot of weight. So I became known as the sickly, scrawny new guy in my class and I wasn't very popular. In fact there was a big bully who made it known that he hated me. In addition to beating me up regularly, he pretty much convinced everyone else that I was somehow tainted. No one wanted to be my friend. No one wanted me to play ball with them. No one invited me to birthday parties. Most everyone agreed that I wasn't worthy to belong. And I thought to myself, *everybody* can't be mistaken. I interpreted the signs to mean I must be worth a pile of crap. You know, children are so good at recording information but they're the worst at knowing how to interpret it. My low self-esteem caused me to exist for years in an unhappy state of bare survival. It was the opposite of thriving. No connection with community, no shared purposes or adventures. I sorely wanted a real life. I knew what life looked like and I wanted it, but I didn't know how to get it."

Manny was staring at his tray table. He looked over to Linda. He noticed compassion on her face and decided to continue. "Later on, as I grew up, I learned to see myself differently. I was blessed to have some incredible people pour life into me and show me my worth. People like my wife Susan, my best friend Noah, my good friends in the Marines—they all helped me learn about how to make life happen. These days, my children teach me about life more than anyone."

He looked Linda dead in the eyes. "You asked why life is important to me. I'll tell you why. It's because I know what it's like to suffocate without it for years. I'm not gonna let that happen to anyone else. Not on my watch. You know, most civilizations have created meaningful community in the places where they worked. Work is one of the most natural places in society to have it."

Linda reached into the seat pocket in front of her and retrieved her notebook computer from between the magazines. "Do you mind if I take some notes here?" She pulled down her tray table and booted up. "I don't want to forget what you've said about leadership."

He shook his head. "I don't mind at all. I'm impressed that you care enough to take notes."

The familiar blank electronic page with a blinking cursor appeared on the screen and she typed:

- **A leader makes life happen for herself and her people because life is the only context that can sustain high performance forever.**
- **Definition of life: a person's optimal state of being (real life begins once all your basic needs are met—when you're thriving, not just surviving).**
- **People encounter life at work as they find their purpose, dive into an adventure, connect with community and create results.**

"By the way," Manny interjected as he looked at the screen, "I like to write the word "Life" with a capital "L" to distinguish it from lesser forms of survival."

"Makes sense." The cursor jumped back through the text and "life" became capitalized. "Manny, would you account for our team's low morale and high turnover by saying that people were not finding Life?"

"Yep." He nodded while a flight attendant walked by with a trash bag. "People aren't finding the Life they're looking for. Everybody always does whatever they think will bring them the most Life." Manny tossed his cup and napkin in the bag. He had an idea. "Give me some names of people who've recently left the firm."

"Okay." Linda rested her chin in her hand. "Pam Weathers and Jay Davenport."

"And where'd they go?"

"Pam is working for a publishing company. And Jay went last month to a venture capital firm in California."

"You see, people always choose whatever they think will bring them the most Life. Obviously they both believed they would find the most Life by making a career move. Now, go ahead and make up a hypothetical story about the missing Life they were seeking."

Linda paused for a moment to think. "Maybe Pam wanted a different kind of challenge or more responsibility. And perhaps Jay needed a lighter travel schedule to give him a chance for more time with his family at home."

"Good. All those things lead to a better Life." Manny decided to press for more. "Now make up a story about the Life motive behind the Venture Capital firm. Why do you think Jay's firm is in the business of investing in start-ups in the first place?"

She was up for the challenge. "The VC partners want profits so they can retire early and fund the Life they really want to live."

"Fantastic. Pam, Jay and the VC partners all have different ways of finding Life, but the pursuit of Life is the common denominator. Thinking about Life this way helps to remind me that Life is an experience that's bigger than all of us. My main responsibility as a leader is to ensure that my people can experience this Life in their work and in each other. All I try to do in my job is to make Life happen. Everything else falls into place when I do this one thing well. Whether I'm encouraging a pod

member or writing a document or researching how to increase
the firm's profits by twenty percent next year—everything I do is
for the sake of furthering Life somehow."

"Aren't you blurring the lines between business and personal
affairs when you try to make Life happen for people?
I mean, what if an associate is having troubles at home with their
marriage or their child's health? These problems could prevent
him from being engaged at work and finding Life there. What's
your responsibility as a manager then?"

"Well, obviously a manager isn't responsible for his associates'
home Life. But the supposed clear line between business and
personal affairs is a myth in some cases. We're whole people.
You can't neatly divide someone's Life into pieces and assume
that the sections don't influence each other. We all bring some of
our work issues home and we also bring some of our home issues
to work. If I have a talented employee who's not living up to his
potential at work due to reasons at home, I may just take
a chance, get personal and try to make Life happen for him.
Or I may choose not to. It's a gray area that I'd have to discern on
a case-by-case basis."

Linda had a doubtful look on her face. It wasn't that she
didn't like Manny's answer. She very much liked what she was
hearing and the fact scared her. This weird man was so radically
different from every other executive she'd known. How could he
be right?

Manny continued. "Life is the reason we do everything in
business. Think of any business endeavor. You'll find the pursuit
of Life as its ultimate inspiration."

Though she hated to admit it, it all made sense to her.
Investing, marketing campaigns, trade conferences, financial
reports and widget manufacturing—all these transactions
happened to maximize the Life available to key constituencies
like customers, employees or investors. By design, someone's Life
benefited every time.

He nodded again. "Life is the ultimate motive of the human race. People will always do whatever they think will bring them the most Life. If they see that following your lead brings them the most Life, then they'll do that. Using that knowledge to move your venture forward is what distinguishes a wise leader from a foolish one."

Manny looked conspiratorially at Linda. "One more thing: of course, as a leader, you never purposely try to fail, but I've found that if you get the Life thing right, you can actually afford to mess up sometimes. Your people will forgive you. Life really is the most important thing they need from you."

The keys on the keyboard clacked, and text appeared on the computer screen:

- **A wise leader moves her company forward by using the knowledge that her people will always do whatever they think will bring them the most Life.**
- **If you turn work into an opportunity to find Life, your people will dive into work with more passion and generate better results.**
- **If you get the one thing (Life) right, when you mess up, people will still follow you.**

"Let me tell you about Terrance." Passion was shining through Manny's words. "I once did a consulting gig in an insurance company and met an employee named Terrance. He was one of those rising stars who really loved his job. He worked in the marketing department for disability insurance policies. He gave everything he had to give, and then some. One day, I invited Terrance to lunch. I asked him why he cared about his work so much.

"He told me that when he was five years old, his father started missing work at his factory job every now and then because of a mysterious illness. The doctors tested him and diagnosed him with multiple sclerosis. Eventually he became paralyzed partially and had to stop working for good. Terrance told me that if it weren't for the proceeds from his dad's disability insurance policy, the family never would have made it. They would have lost their house. They would've barely seen their mother since she would have been working at least two shifts to make ends meet. Terrance probably wouldn't have gone to college. You see, the insurance made it possible for their family to find Life. So Terrance grew up caring about families being protected by insurance.

"And that's why Terrance has a hidden advantage at work. Every time he creates a new marketing campaign for a disability insurance product, he experiences a surge of Life that no one else in his office can duplicate. He has the same responsibilities and the same boss as other people on his team, but he has a secret power source. Where other people find work, he finds Life. Life produces enough initiative and endurance in him to overcome every obstacle. The last I heard, he was getting promoted."

Gears were turning in Linda's mind. "If a CEO could take Terrance's power source and put it inside all her employees, the company would blow all the competition away."

"That's why we can never forget that our number one job as a leader is to protect and advance the Life of our people. They don't need the same childhood that Terrance had. They need someone to give them an environment where they can find Life. I've seen companies filled with people who work like Terrance. Life is a company's competitive advantage. It's what gives your people the passion they need to break through the obstacles that are bound to come."

Linda typed:

- **As a leader protects and advances the Life of her people, she empowers them to make**

breakthrough results happen. It's so simple that it's easy to forget. So remember: real leadership brings Life, which in turn makes breakthroughs happen.

Linda eventually decided to catch up on current events from the in-flight TV news program. She pressed the touch screen on the seatback facing her. Manny reclined in his seat and closed his eyes. The captain announced that the flight had started its descent.

Manny opened his eyes a moment later. "I think I'm realizing something for the first time: simplicity is the reason why Life is such a powerful idea. I mean it's a simple concept that helps me make complex leadership decisions." Manny caught himself. "I'm probably boring you as I ramble here. Sorry."

"No. Please continue." She seemed earnest.

Manny shifted in his seat, glad to continue. "When you look at an Olympic athlete performing, or a talented musician, you realize that all the brightest stars are people who've mastered the fundamentals of their discipline. Well, leadership is no different. The problem is that vast numbers of us forget to concentrate on the basics. We focus on the cosmetic rather than on the core."

"By the core of leadership, you mean escorting your people into their optimal state of being?"

"Yeah. That's what's at the core of being a good leader. It takes courage to lead from the core, but it produces singular results. Today's business landscape is more complex than ever before. A lot of the leadership books and seminars teach you how to handle the complexity by throwing an assortment of tips and techniques at you. Lots of helpful insights, but they don't offer any core organizing principle to help you filter through all the information."

"I know what you mean. You come away with a lot of strategies but you never feel like you know, deep in your heart, what it takes to be a good leader."

"The way to become a great leader is not to focus on the tips and techniques. You just have to remember the main target: to make Life happen for your people and your mission. You can only afford to dwell on tips and techniques after you've mastered the basics of a Life-giving leadership style. Do you mind helping me come up with a few of these tips and techniques?"

"No problem." Linda opened her computer and clicked over to the document with her leadership notes from before. The two brainstormed about some of the techniques that were necessary to be an effective leader. Linda created a bullet point list as they spoke:

- Set forth a clear vision
- Gain the commitment of people
- Define expectations clearly
- Take charge
- Don't take charge and let your group learn how to make better decisions
- Get a close-up picture of the front lines
- Get the big picture
- Be a talent developer
- Balance multiple stakeholders' needs and points of view
- Give good feedback
- Seek feedback from others
- Manage conflict
- Pay attention to advice
- Pay no attention to advice
- Be forceful
- Be gentle

- Empower your people
- Hold people accountable
- Be detail-oriented but don't be a control freak
- Bring all your technical skills to bear on issues
- Leave your technical skills behind to focus on managing people

"These are just a few of the skills and techniques a leader has to use," Manny said, "and there are literally hundreds more of them in the leadership literature. Too many to remember. What we need is a simpler way."

Linda recalled the leadership seminar that Human Resources had arranged for the associates a few months before. She struggled to think of one single thing from the seminar that she had applied consistently since then. "I see what you're saying. There are lots of skills to remember. It's like having a hundred tools in a big toolbox. It's nice, but if you don't choose your tools correctly, you end up building a mess."

Manny then spoke of an experience he had years ago as a summer intern. "My boss that summer gave me an impossibly complex project on my first day at work. As if that weren't enough, he gave me an impossibly short deadline too. He took only a few seconds to describe the hairy assignment and he used cryptic language. I was very confused so I asked him to clarify some details and to point me in the right direction. He looked at me with a smile and said, 'You're a smart guy. Figure it out for yourself.' He then stared at me with a knowing look as if to say, 'You'll thank me later.'"

"He thought he was teaching you to be independent and resourceful, but he didn't prepare you enough to accomplish the task," Linda surmised.

"Exactly. I spent almost twenty-four hours feverishly working and dreading that I wouldn't be able to finish the project. No one else in our unit was available to help me. I felt like a colossal failure. Finally, with the deadline looming, I turned to a colleague in another unit and asked for help."

Linda was perturbed. "Your boss took the wrong skills out of the toolbox. He set you up for failure while he thought he was doing the opposite. You don't leave interns alone to find complex solutions on day one."

"You got it. If my boss had picked some supportive tools out of the toolbox, like mentoring or directing, then I could have found Life in my relationship with him. I would have seen working with him as an opportunity to find Life and I would have wanted to do more work for him. Instead, I quickly learned that I couldn't trust my manager to support me in taking new ground or to protect me from arbitrarily tight deadlines. I couldn't trust him for my Life. As things worked out that summer, I found a way to become attached to some different projects that were led by someone else. I ditched Mr. You'll-Thank-Me-Later and chose another mentor who brought me Life. You see, Life is what makes you loyal to a leader."

Linda typed quickly as they wrapped up their conversation. She was trying to evade the evil eye of the flight attendant patrolling for electronic devices not yet shut down for landing. Linda recorded Manny's points and added some thoughts of her own:

- **Life is what makes a leader attractive to people. People give their loyalty to leaders who consistently provide Life.**
- **You can tinker with leadership tips and techniques forever, but you'll never accomplish anything significant through your team until you choose to make Life happen for your people and your mission.**

- **Some executives derail their careers by not knowing how to use the correct tools at the correct time. Sometimes they keep their leadership positions, but end up failing at Life. They stay in their jobs only because their companies are too shortsighted to care that they are poor leaders.**

- **So how do you know which leadership skills to apply in a given situation? Simply think about Life when you reach into the toolbox. Ask yourself, "How can I use my skills to create the most Life in this situation?"**

She saved her document, powered off the machine and closed the computer in time to catch the inquiring stare of the flight attendant hovering over her. Linda's face lit up with an innocent smile.

❖   ❖   ❖

CHAPTER SIX

The door to Jack's office was closed later that afternoon. Manny approached it and hesitated, debating whether to knock or come back later. He spun around to face Rachel's desk.

Rachel was the feisty fifty-two-year-old administrative assistant assigned to both Jack and Manny. Her cubicle was right across the hallway from Jack's office and a few paces down from Manny's. Rachel was Manny's go-to gal for matters of firm etiquette, firm politics, office supplies or even the best restaurants within a five-block radius. She was quite the encyclopedia. Increasingly, she was also proving to be quite the meteorologist.

She spoke softly, "So you want the weather report?" Her eyes squinted with delight. "It's stormy. The prospective client in Seattle didn't bite. That's the third one this month, so it's definitely stormy." Rachel enjoyed speaking in code about Jack's temperament. It usually passed as the second most exciting part of her day. The real excitement was whenever she could sneak a swig of vodka from the thermos hidden in the bottom drawer of her desk. Everyone appreciated the large bowl of breath mints on her desk.

Manny grabbed a mint, mouthed the word "thanks" and went back to his office. He would wait.

Tom Walker, one of the associates, hailed Manny from down the hall. He had come by to find out how the Joval presentation went. He couldn't wait until the 4:30 pod meeting for the news. Tom was one of those witty, slightly overweight technical geniuses that no operation can do without. On a good day, his sandy hair was just slightly messy and only half of his shirt was sticking out from his trousers. The two went into Manny's office and chatted. As Manny was relaying the details about the triumph in Boston, he heard Jack come out of his office and generate the usual muted drone reserved for speaking with Rachel.

"Tom, I hear Jack down the hall. Do you mind if I fill you in on the rest at the meeting?"

"No problem." Tom excused himself.

Manny trotted down the hall. Jack had already disappeared. Before he could open his mouth, Rachel replied, "In the library." She didn't bother to look up from her typing.

Manny walked through cubicle land. He greeted some of the young analysts on the way. He passed by the Xerox/vending machine room where the associates convened to make copies and glare at each other's shoes with envy. He glided through the entrance of the firm library and past the glossy new magazines. He walked straight through to the boring section in the back left. Bingo. Jack was sitting at one of the desks, texting someone. His face was long.

"May I join you?" Manny asked.

Jack was taken aback. After gathering his thoughts, he said, "Have a seat."

"I was thinking you might want to take the reins at the 4:30 pod meeting. It's been a while since the whole group's seen you up front and it'll be great for the pod to celebrate our victory."

Jack worked to put on a smile and looked up. "I don't think I'm going to make it. You handle the meeting. I've got to make some more calls."

Jack knew that Lee and Adam had recently stayed up late to help Manny. He'd heard the glowing reports of how Manny had ushered the pod into a new level of teamwork. He'd seen even Linda become all smiles around Manny. Why was he so agitated by Manny's overnight popularity with the pod? He wanted Manny to do well, but not that well.

"You okay?" Manny asked.

"I'm fine."

"No. How are you really doing?"

"I'm really fine." There was an edge of finality in his second "fine."

Manny had hit a conversational brick wall. It was the first time he knew for sure something was wrong. He'd noticed a disconnect several times before, but he'd always chalked it up to the busyness of firm life, or Jack wearing his I-have-to-be-the-boss hat, or Jack just having a bad day. Manny did a quick inventory in his memory. Had he inadvertently done something to upset Jack? No. Not likely. Perhaps the storm would blow over in time. Manny and Jack's carefree days at Columbia University suddenly seemed so long ago.

Linda passed through the turnstile and exited the Clark Street subway station. Her feet were aching as they always did after a long day of work and travel, but she didn't mind. Once out into the evening, she was greeted by the familiar tree-lined streets of her neighborhood. The air in Brooklyn Heights was alive with the sounds of families and the occasional helicopter flying overhead.

She stopped in the little store on the corner of Henry and Clark streets and picked up some popcorn and a newspaper. She headed for the cashier and became the seventh person in line. She glanced around mischievously before opening the popcorn and partaking. Four customers later, the bag was half empty. When she arrived at the counter, she confessed, "Couldn't wait." Jamal, the storeowner, looked at her with kind eyes while shaking his head. "Again," she added with a smile, tucking a few strands of hair behind her ear.

There was an atypical lightness in her steps as she continued the walk home. She had the grace of someone who was comfortable in her skin. She almost felt like a little girl again. If she could have spun around in a twirly skirt right there, she would have. She realized that for the first time in ages that she was unexpectedly happy. Today had been a landmark day in the world of Linda Flores.

She had doubted Manny long enough. He seemed to put his money where his mouth was, so she would trust him—a little bit—for now at least. If he morphed into some monster later on, she reserved the right to write him off. But for now, he had done everything humanly possible to extend a true hand of friendship. She would choose to enjoy the moment. After all, most elusive things like trust and joy were a choice.

But why was she having to make this choice several times per minute? Why was it still so hard for her to believe that Manny would continue being as good as he seemed to be? She knew the answer to the question as soon as she asked herself. Her father had been in and out of her childhood like the sun on a cloudy day. She didn't talk too much about her Papi these days—the man with perennial whiskers and a taste for chess. He's the reason why Linda developed an early appreciation for strategy. For many years, the caustic opinions he shouted when drunk had precluded Linda's chance to grow her own.

Nevertheless, the forcefulness of his presence around the house was not nearly as painful as his absence. She could count on one hand the years that he'd lived at home with her. He stayed for sixteen whole calendar months once when they were living in Miami. That all-time record was the last time she ever saw him.

She was twelve at the time. She'd never been good about trusting people since then.

Yet, against all odds, something was new about her today. She was more ready to trust than she'd been in a while. She reminded herself that trust was a choice. She resolved to make the choice as many times per minute as it took to give this new boss a try. Even if he'd taken the job she'd wanted.

She finished the bag of popcorn, fished inside her purse for her keys and opened the front door of her apartment building. No one else was in the lobby. She extracted her mail through the tiny mailbox door and, without thinking, twirled on her tiptoes.

PART THREE

❖   ❖   ❖

The Proposal

❖   ❖   ❖

CHAPTER SEVEN

A painted sky of gold, orange and pink on canvas. A golden ridge of trees ablaze with the brilliance of the sunrise. The frame was golden too. Upon joining Cyrus & Hopkins, all new managers and partners had the option of displaying a piece from the firm's art collection in their offices. Manny chose a landscape.

This particular painting would lend a nice aesthetic to his office. It was high time for his office to look more "lived in." Two very busy months had elapsed since his first day at the firm. The room was badly in need of some color. The only item hanging on his otherwise bare walls was a small wooden plaque by the filing cabinet that read:

> *"Let us put*
> *our minds together*
> *and see*
> *what Life we can make*
> *for our children."*
> —Sitting Bull

Manny directed the two maintenance men to hang the large painting over the couch in the conference area. He thanked them as they left. He lounged against his desk and tried to determine if there was enough light for the painting in that location. Yes, there was. He lingered for a moment and closed his eyes. He imagined himself inside the painting, taking in the beauty of the grandiose sunrise with the grass and trees before him. He was in a place of infinite possibilities. He liked it.

He opened his eyes again and viewed the actual painting. He was considering the firm's great attention to office décor when a new thought intruded. What if the firm paid this much attention to the interior design of their people too? Perhaps then the "exemplary organization" described on the firm's website wouldn't feel like such a sham.

"A fine choice, sweetheart." Rachel had walked up to the door and noticed him admiring the painting. It was always good to see Rachel. She had become even more of a resource for Manny than before. She had the perfect vantage point to observe him in action with the associates and Jack. She found his authenticity a refreshing change at the firm.

Once there was a political skirmish at a firm-wide meeting of partners and managers. Divisions fell along the classical lines of alliance, with the participating (voting) partners on one side and the non-participating managers on the other. Manny publicly defended Jack and consequently took flak from his fellow managers, who questioned his judgment. Rachel later asked Manny why he had defended Jack at such personal risk. "Because he was right," was his reply.

At lunch, the secretarial assistants were in the habit of chatting with each other about their bosses. One day, when it was Rachel's turn, she equated Manny to a happy-go-lucky teenager with the wisdom of a seventy-year-old. "The other day at a meeting, Manny answered one of Deborah Hopkins's questions by saying, 'I don't know. I'll look into it and get back to you tomorrow.'"

Rachel turned her palms face up to underscore her amazement. "Can you believe it? No one admits to not knowing things. Manny seems so simple but he's a mystery. You just can't resist watching him Forrest-Gump his way through battles. You know he's going to win, but you never know how."

The pod started broadcasting the benefits of Mannydom too, particularly to the associates in the other pods. Overnight, the Blue Pod had become known as the "fun pod." Word spread about Manny's rascally playfulness that was always looking for a good moment to be unleashed. Laughter frequently punctuated Blue Pod meetings and helped the associates not to take themselves too seriously.

Little by little, the pod members began to trust Manny to care for them. Consequently, they allowed him to stretch them in ways they would never allow anyone else to. They took on personally risky assignments that expanded their capacities to manage projects and lead people. Manny even had some of the senior associates leading pod meetings on a rotating basis (this raised a few eyebrows in the other pods). After the associates facilitated their assigned meetings, he gave them plain feedback on what was great and what needed improvement. As a result, the associates felt more of a sense of ownership in the pod and became better equipped to make results happen.

With all the real signs of improvement going on inside the pod, a significant problem lurked just outside; there weren't enough new clients in the pipeline for the months ahead. The associates had plenty of work to keep them busy for now, but everyone knew that more clients would be needed soon. Most of the pods at Cyrus & Hopkins were in the same boat. New clients were harder to come by than ever before. Increased competition in the consulting industry accounted for part of the new pressures, but the worsening economy was the factor that most dampened the mood of the firm's partners.

Deborah Hopkins even took the unprecedented step of asking the firm's associates to participate in the quest for prospective clients. This was semi-controversial since the associates didn't receive any financial incentives for bringing in new business. In the midst of this climate, Manny became concerned for Jack. He could tell that Jack feared losing his reputation as a leading rainmaker.

Rachel sighed and headed toward her desk. "I have to finish the time reports before Mount Saint Jack erupts."

"Is he treating you well?" Manny asked.

She flashed a telling look. "That which does not kill me only makes me complain more." She walked off, adding, "But it's relatively sunny today."

Armed with an update on the weather, Manny gathered his gumption. It was time to talk to Jack about a potential new client: an operator of a chain of restaurants around greater New York City. It would be a modest project compared to the size of the firm's typical client case, but the opportunity had potential to be a gateway to a much larger assignment with implications far beyond the Tri-State area.

As Manny walked down the corridor, he shook his head briefly, trying to forget his disappointment in Jack. Manny had asked Jack to lunch a few times each week during his first month at the firm. There was always a good excuse why Jack had to turn him down. The frequency of Manny's attempts declined somewhat in his second month until he finally resolved not to ask anymore. It became too embarrassing to watch Jack try to manufacture new ways to veil his indifference. Two months, and the storm over their friendship had not dissipated.

Why didn't they have real conversations anymore? Granted, Jack was often traveling, trying to woo new clients. But even when he was in the office, he was never available. Whenever the two did manage to talk, it was simply to cover the essentials for the pod's work. Occasionally, after talking shop, a short spell of chitchat would transpire. Very occasionally. There were no hints from Jack as to what had happened. Manny had his theories, but he couldn't tell for sure. Was it just that Jack was jealous?

Jack of course knew that Manny had been fishing for more meaningful interactions, but Jack was in no mood for chummy time. In a small way, he felt sorry for Manny. He knew Manny would never get what he was fishing for. It was hard for Jack to feel good around Manny, even if Manny hadn't done anything wrong that Jack could point to. And Jack had definitely tried pointing.

As Manny approached Rachel's desk, her telephone rang and she answered, "Good morning, Jack Jameson's office." A pause. "I'll be glad to check and see if he's available, but you really should call him 'Mr. Jameson.' Calling him 'the guru' won't do." Another silence, and the caller obviously must have let Rachel know that he was a potential client. "I understand, just one moment. I'll put you through to Mr. Guru."

Manny hovered around Rachel's desk, engaging in small talk for a minute or two while Jack wrapped things up on the phone. From the tone of Jack's voice, Manny could tell the prospective client was not interested in hiring the firm. Once the call was over, Manny knocked on the door and entered the office. "Hi."

Jack was writing something on a pad of sticky notes. He looked up. "Are you planning on living in Queens forever? Pretty much all the partners live in Manhattan or Connecticut. You can afford it now."

Manny sat down. "I know, but Susan and I like the community in Sunnyside. We're fine in Queens. Can I talk about a potential client?"

"Talk." Jack had a poker face. His voice was perky but his eyes never danced anymore.

"Are you familiar with Osanto's Bar & Grill around the corner?"

"Sure."

"Well as you probably know, they're part of a chain in the Tri-State area. At Rachel's suggestion, I've eaten there a few times. Good food. I met the president of the chain there once. Richard Delgado. We struck up a conversation and exchanged business cards. We played phone tag for a while but we finally spoke yesterday and he got excited when I brought up the idea of us working for them."

Manny was grateful to be able to bring some good news to the table. Maybe this project would be something he and Jack could work on together. "He wants us to give him a quote for a marketing research project. To keep up with the latest New York City laws, they're in the process of reformulating their menu to be one hundred percent trans-fat free. Since they're going to have to change their menu to some degree, they're thinking that now may be a good time for some additional changes to increase their market share. We can add a fresh perspective and help them identify the right changes for their target market."

"It's not the sexiest project, but it's work," Jack replied. "How many restaurants do they have?"

"Sixteen, but here's the best part: Osanto's is a subsidiary of a holding company with over five hundred restaurants nation-wide and some holdings abroad too. It's called Osanto Restaurants International. This guy, Richard, has major pull with the holding company since his restaurants are the most profitable chain in the collection. And he gave me his word that he'd open the door for us to work with a nationwide initiative that the hold-ing company's doing. He told me, confidentially, that he's about to be tapped to lead the initiative."

"Manny, I know this seems exciting but there's no way we can work on such a small scale. Sixteen units is way too small for us. We have other projects to focus on. The way we make money is by going for the big boys. Big clients, big money. I'd be happy to talk with the guy about the nationwide initiative, but we can't do small potatoes."

Manny wasn't ready to give up. "I've tried that route with Richard already. He's been burned with some bad experiences with consultants before. He likes me but he insisted on seeing whether we can deliver on a smaller project first. I don't blame him. If we're as good as I said we are, he'll open the door to the national deal. He gave me his word."

Jack had already moved on. He was reading a newspaper on his desk. "You'll learn. Nothing good comes from jumping through hoops and I can't spare the pod's resources to chase a mirage." He looked up to make his final point. "Either we take the national case or no deal."

Manny swallowed, willing himself to rise above the chill of Jack's ultimatum.

Jack looked down at his papers again. "Oh, and on your way out, remind Rachel that I'll need to have the binders by tomorrow."

Anger pumped through Manny's veins. A huge opportunity was slipping away. Manny tried to generate the required sparkle in his tone. "Jack, you're underestimating this opportunity because it's coming in a humble form." Manny walked out the door and reminded Rachel about the binders.

❖   ❖   ❖

CHAPTER EIGHT

I f things with Jack had grown worse over time, things with
Linda had improved. The Boston surprise had put an end to
her awkward, halting disposition with Manny. She still didn't
trust him completely, but it seemed they were on the road to
friendship.

The next day, Adam and Linda sauntered out of the Xerox/
vending machine room armed with snacks. Linda threw a mini-
pretzel up in the air and caught it in her mouth. As Adam noted
her cheeriness, she confided, "I asked Manny to teach me about
leadership and today's our first meeting."

Adam recalled the pod meeting when Manny had invited
everyone who wanted to learn more about leadership to stop by
his office and chat. Adam was curious, but not enough to stop
by Manny's office. "Let me know how it goes," he told Linda.
"I was thinking of doing the same thing myself, but I can't afford
the time right now. I've got too much work to do. What made you
decide to go for it?"

"I never met a boss before whose success rides on his
people feeling alive. He cares about both people and results.
That's a rare combination."

Adam stuffed a cheesy-puff stick into his mouth and wondered whether perhaps he should make some time to talk to Manny too.

Later that day, Linda approached Manny's office with notebook computer in hand. She stopped at the open door when she saw Susan and Manny sitting on the couch, holding hands and talking.

"Hi Linda. Come on in." Manny motioned to Linda.

"Hello," Linda replied.

"This is my wife, Susan." They rose from the couch.

After the handshake, Susan kissed Manny on the cheek and headed toward the door. "I was just on my way out. I don't want to make you two late for your first leadership session."

Linda shook her head. "You're not holding us up at all. As a matter of fact, I'm a couple minutes early. I guess I was eager to learn how to lead like your husband does."

Susan smiled and looked at Linda. "He's got a thing or two to share. It's good to meet you." She then shared a glance with Manny and waved goodbye. Walking down the hallway, she remembered the first time she had dared to stare into Manny's golden eyes for more than a few seconds. It had been fourteen years ago. She had instantly wanted to shrink back from the love and authority she saw in his eyes. She would have retreated too, except that she couldn't stop staring. Yeah, he's a keeper, she thought to herself.

Linda walked over to a chair and sat down to set up her laptop on the coffee table. "So, in our conversation on the plane," she stopped to make sure the computer was booting up properly, "we discussed the idea that Life is what motivates people to perform at breakthrough levels. So a leader's got to maximize the Life they can access."

"Right."

"Well, if Life is so crucial, why doesn't anybody talk about it except you?"

Manny, who had plunked himself onto the couch, was smiling. "Good question." He was looking at the painting of the sunrise when he spoke. "It's true. Most people don't talk about it as much as I do, but that doesn't mean they aren't relying on Life to lead. There are literally millions of smart people who've aligned themselves with Life to make leadership decisions every-day. A lot of them are a part of the organization with the best track record for producing Life. In fact, it's the world's most important organization. Care to offer a guess as to what it is?"

She scooted back a little in her chair and shook her head.

He went on, "It's the family. Where would any of us be without it? Families are great places to pick up best practices about leading with Life. Unlike a corporation, the family organization exists exclusively for the purpose of protecting and advancing the Life of its members. Over the millennia that this organization has been around, a lot of families have become proficient in giving Life to their members. Not all families are healthy families, but there are enough great ones out there for us to learn from.

"So we have on one hand, a lot of families thriving, while on the other hand we have masses of workers in business, govern-ment and nonprofits starving for Life. What's needed here? It's simple. We need leaders who can bridge the gap between the family and the marketplace. Whenever I can, I try to bring best practices from home to create Life at work. I try to consider how I make Life happen for my wife and children and then I translate it for my colleagues in the office."

A smirk crept across Linda's face. It all sounded so innocent and yet so subversive. You never knew what to expect from Manny. Still, she had questions. "Don't you run the risk of being labeled paternalistic if you treat your employees like your kids? After all, we're supposed to be surrounded by adults here and no one wants their boss acting like Mommy or Daddy." Halfway through saying it, she felt a little regret. Hopefully Manny wouldn't think that she saw him as paternalistic.

It didn't seem to faze him. "It surely would be paternalistic to treat employees like kids, making all the decisions for them and holding their hands all the time. But that's not what I'm talking about. I hope you can tell that I treat my kids and my office colleagues very differently. But I also hope you can see that my motives for leading at work and at home are identical. Motives are everything. My motive is always to maximize Life."

"Remind me again what your definition of Life is. I mean, what's your definition of Life at work rather than Life at home."

"Life is your optimal state of being. The definition is the same for both work and home, even though you'll customize the way you make it happen in each place. Life is the natural overflow that happens in people when they find a meaningful purpose, go on an adventure and create real results in the context of a true community. The overflow looks like thriving and it takes place in every human being, from kids at home to associates at work. Life is the only context in which you can sustain high performance forever.

"For a leader, having a Life motive means you're motivated to see your people thrive and not just survive at home and at work. Your motive has to be consistent whether you're in the living room or the boardroom because Life works everywhere. Human nature doesn't change from room to room, so why would you ever shift your strategy for bringing out the best in others?"

Manny got up and strolled to the window. He slid his hands into his pockets as he spoke. "It's important that my family, friends and work colleagues can *all* count on me for Life. It doesn't matter if the person in front of me is wearing an Armani suit, a janitor's uniform or diapers. It doesn't matter whether I meet them in my living room or in my office. What matters is that I've chosen to be the kind of guy who makes Life happen, period."

Manny took in the pathways meandering through Central Park, twenty-five stories below his window. He spotted something. "Those two guys down there can teach us something."

Linda joined him by the window. He pointed toward one of the park entrances off of 59th Street. She could barely make out the form of a man walking with a young child about two or three years old. "Are you pointing at the man with the child?"

He nodded. "Let's pick up a best practice from a leader in that family organization. Let's make up a story about that Dad. The mission of his little organization is to protect and maximize the Life of its members, so let's see how Dad lives out that mission through his decisions. Let's say the toddler woke up today and Dad changed his diapers. After all, it's hard to thrive when you're walking around with loaded diapers. After that, Dad made breakfast to energize the child's Life that day."

Joy flickered across Manny's eyes. "I'm calling the son Peter. Yeah. So next, Dad takes little Pete to Central Park and pushes him on the swings to give him a high quality of Life. Later they go exploring through the playground and Dad drops behind by ten feet to let Pete explore the park a little on his own. Why? Because Pete will need to develop self-confidence if he's going to make it in Life. Then, at one point, Dad suddenly sprints to catch up with Pete, to stop him from running gleefully into the busy street next to the park. Dad saves the child's Life. Finally Dad takes his son home for naptime since rest is an important part of Life. You get the gist."

Linda tracked the father and child walking below and said, "He applies just one standard, Life, to the countless decisions he makes throughout the day for the sake of his follower."

"Exactly. A good leader doesn't mix and match his Life motive with other self-serving motives based upon his emotions. Dad ruthlessly goes after one thing all day long. He's quite predictable, and that makes Pete glad because that means Dad is a dependable source of Life. A good family leader lives out one standard alone by the imposition of his will, because it's the only thing that works over time for his organization."

Linda realized too that being a source of Life had the side effect of producing huge amounts of loyalty in the family organization. It was the same kind of loyalty that the Blue Pod associates were beginning to feel for their leader and each other.

Manny tapped the window with his finger for emphasis as he spoke. "This is the way it has to be for leaders in education, government, soy farming or any industry. It's not difficult to understand how to lead with Life. A good leader ruthlessly focuses on how to maximize Life as she makes countless leadership decisions every day. To make breakthrough results happen, your people have to trust you for Life. Just like a family leader, your ambition has to be primarily for the Life of your organization, and not yourself. You really don't have to look out for yourself as much as you'd think because you experience Life as you make it happen for others."

Linda thought about her childhood spent between Panama and the United States. Linda suddenly felt queasy as she pondered the painful absence of her father. Papi made more misery happen than Life, she thought. She wondered if Manny, lost in his world of exemplary families, could even relate.

"I think most kids understand that Life's the ultimate standard." Manny sighed. Vapor appeared on the cold window. "But then we grow up. We go to work in our first jobs and promptly leave our Life motive at home. We let a corporate culture dictate what we personally value. Why do we do that?"

He turned around to lean on the glass. He looked at Linda. She was silent, so he went on thinking aloud. "I think we do it because we want to get ahead in the organization and because we're scared to do otherwise. We let our responsibility to make Life happen become some distant, optional notion the moment we step into an office building. All of a sudden, we adopt a different set of standards and we never question whether the office standards are right. But they're dead wrong. Most corporate cultures are painfully devoid of Life. These organizations offer the promise of Life, but it's an empty promise. And this is our own fault, isn't it? We've invited these cultures since we're too frightened to get personal—too afraid that things could get messy. We keep our colleagues at arm's length because it's easier than taking the risk of putting ourselves out there and getting stepped on. And this sterile arrangement is what's accepted as normal today. Well, not everyone believes that normal is good."

"Manny?"

His reverie was broken. "Yes."

"Can I be honest with you?"

"Please do."

"My childhood wasn't the greatest. I can't draw on a whole bunch of best practices from my home. This family model may work fine for you, but all it does is make me feel like crap."

Manny felt a swell of compassion and regretted his insensitivity. He'd been pontificating about the beauty of the family without thinking about whether Linda could draw from a similar bank account of pleasant family memories. He looked in her eyes. "I'm sorry if I made it seem as if everybody's family was ideal. All of us have some not-so-pretty parts in our family life. That's what it means to be human. I've got some real crazies in my extended family. We only let them out of the attic for family reunions." He laughed. "But, even if your family was dysfunctional, you need to know that today you have what it takes to lead from the perspective of Life. You're not doomed to repeat the mistakes of your family."

Linda sighed. "But I don't know what the Life-giving thing to do is in every situation."

"Neither do I. Don't worry about it. All you need is a willingness to discover how to make Life happen. No matter what your background was, today you can observe the world around you for signs of Life. Just be on the lookout for healthy bosses, teams, families, friendships or marriages. Remember that true Life looks like thriving. So look anywhere you see people thriving and try to figure out why so much Life is showing up in that context. I'll sometimes go up to a manager at one of our client sites and ask them, 'What are you doing that's making your team thrive so much?'"

Linda sighed, "But half the time, I don't know what Life looks like."

"Linda."

"Yes."

"You'll recognize Life when you see it because you're a human being. So long as you're looking for it, then you'll recognize it when you find yourself or someone else thriving."

Linda still had reservations, but she smiled. Manny was glad to see her smiling.

They headed back to the discussion area. She typed out:

- **Bring your best practices from home to create Life at work.**
- **The leader at home and the leader at work may use different behaviors, but they must have identical motives: to make Life happen.**
- **Distinguish yourself as one who has ambition for the Life of your organization, and not yourself. You experience Life as you give it to others, so you don't have to look out for yourself as much as you'd think.**
- **Regardless of your background, everyone can and must be a student of Life. Observe the healthy relationships around you for signs of Life. Do the work of finding out why Life is showing up in those contexts.**

As she was typing the last line, she asked, "Manny, what are some of the best practices you've brought from home and translated for the office?"

He sat down on a chair. "One thing I learned was that Susan needed me to show her that I would always be by her side. In my own mind, I always had been by her side, but at first I didn't realize how necessary it was to show her that truth with my words and actions. One time, Susan had a verbally abusive colleague in her office. She would come home feeling deflated every night. She tried talking to the man, but he pretended that there was nothing to talk about. She was debating whether to say something to her boss or not. She didn't want to rock the boat needlessly.

"When Susan talked it over with me, I encouraged her to take a risk and let her boss know what was going on. Susan told me that the conversation might not be worth it because the man and her boss were close friends. I told her, 'You need to talk to your boss about this because you're worth it, no matter what your boss's reaction is. Even if you get transferred or fired because you made a stink, that's okay. I don't care. I'll take care of you.'"

Manny slapped his hand on his forehead to underscore his point. "I'm so glad I supported her. I got to be the straw on the camel's back, so to speak. Susan resolved to have the conversation with her boss, and he took disciplinary action against the colleague. Susan's self-worth grew. Her career eventually thrived because she had developed more self-confidence to stand up for herself. Even my children are thriving because of the self-worth they're now inheriting from my wife. So that's a best practice to make Life happen at work. Your people will constantly worry about whether they're in or out of your graces. Every day, your people will attempt to gauge that. To be an effective leader, you have to consistently plant seeds of inclusion to remind them that they're in. Show your people that they're valuable and that you're on their side. Then, empower your folks to see themselves as leaders when they execute their mission. If everyone sees themselves as a leader who is responsible for making sure the right things happen, then your team's performance will shine in a way no one else can duplicate."

Linda remarked, "Jack often says, 'Our associates are our greatest assets.' But I don't get the sense that he cares much about me as a person. Sometimes I feel like I'm just a cog in his consulting machine. But if he would show me rather than just talking about it, maybe then I'd believe that I'm his greatest asset."

Linda then recalled the words of Manny's speech on his first day of work. He'd made it clear that his primary objective was to remove the obstacles that kept the associates from shining. He set the expectation that he'd be by their side and his actions had proven that his words weren't hollow. Linda's document sprouted three new lines:

- **Life happens when your people know they matter and you're on their side.**
- **Constantly plant seeds of inclusion with your words and, more importantly, your actions.**
- **Empower your people to see themselves as leaders who are responsible for making sure the right things happen when they execute their mission.**

Manny summed things up: "These practices pave the way for your people to trust you. The ultimate in trust happens when your people believe they can consistently find Life by following your lead. Once they can depend on you for their Life, watch out! They'll stand with you, work for you and thrive. They'll knock into oblivion any obstacle that dares to stand between them and their mission."

Linda looked at her watch and realized that it was time for her next appointment. "Apparently, time flies when you're growing wiser."

"Well, we've covered a lot of the basics of leading so far. Next time, we'll discuss a way to make Life multiply exponentially. The truly great leaders in human history all adopted a singular way to achieve breakthrough results through their people. I'm looking forward to our next conversation when we can dive into it."

Linda protested in laughter. "Leaving me with a cliff-hanger, are you?"

"I'll tell you this much for now: a good leader makes Life happen by blending two personal traits into one."

CHAPTER NINE

Noah and Manny ran at top speed across multiple lanes of traffic on the circular road that surrounded the statue. A flock of pigeons on the sidewalk dispersed into the sky as the men arrived at the curb. They sat down with their bagged lunches on a bench by the statue of Columbus in the middle of Columbus Circle. It was sublime to be back in the sun again, even if it was only fifty-two degrees.

They were still a little winded from the run. "Hey, man, you're out of breath," Manny teased through his own panting.

"Maybe I am, but why are *you* breathing so hard? I'm not the one who gets up at the crack of dawn to jog every morning."

"That was in my twenties, when I believed I was the type of guy who got up at five to jog."

Noah lifted the end of Manny's tie and inspected its swirl pattern. "It appears your tie survived from your twenties."

"You don't get it," Manny said flatly while reaching into his sandwich bag.

"Get what?" He dropped the tie.

"I'm wearing it *ironically*." Manny bit into his tuna sandwich with lettuce and mustard. "How are things going at work?"

Noah reached into his bag and pulled out a salad in a plastic bowl. "I've started to mentor the two new guys we hired last week. We're in the fun stage now. They're starting to know the ropes and they're hungry to make a difference. They're becoming curious about the Life they see in my leadership. Hopefully, we'll be able to talk about it more in the weeks ahead like you're doing with Linda." Manny appreciated having a friend who understood the ways of Life.

Noah rested his fork on his salad. "I can't do this." He reached into his paper bag with his free hand. Out came a hot dog. "Time for dessert." After a few bites, the conversation turned to Manny's work. "How'd things go with that restaurant chain?"

"Don't ask."

"What? The guy isn't interested in hiring your firm anymore?"

"It's worse. Jack vetoed the project because it's too small a deal. I told him about the national project Richard intends to give us, but Jack's not even willing to investigate it. He doesn't want to pull the pod away from paying gigs to chase what he calls 'a mirage.' He told me it's either the national deal or no deal."

Noah put down his hot dog. "Sorry to hear that. As a matter of fact, I'm sorry that things have gotten so messed up with Jack and you recently. It's not right. You've been giving him the best you've got. Want me to go beat him up?"

Manny coughed a few times before he could laugh. The abrupt remark had almost made his soda go down the wrong pipe. He finally eked out, "I'll keep your offer in mind." Even though Noah was only joking, it was comforting to know that someone was on his side.

Noah had the same thoughtful look he always got when trying to put words to ideas. Manny waited for the outcome.

"Maybe there's a creative way for you to go after Osanto's without pulling the entire pod away from the other projects."

"How?"

"That's what I was about to ask you. How could you make that happen?"

Gears turned in Manny's mind. Perhaps there was a way to do the introductory project after all. He took a long stroll back to work when lunchtime was over, contemplating along the way. He was grinning as he passed through the revolving doors into the lobby of the building. When no one was looking, he took a running start from the welcome carpet and slid a few feet across the polished floor in his black leather shoes.

It was a Friday evening at seven o'clock and Conference Room A, the firm's largest and most posh room, buzzed with the sounds of merrymaking. Food and drinks were available on most every table. The central table had an ice sculpture of the Joval logo. The Blue Pod was hosting a firm-wide celebration of the Joval Financial Group's recent success. The bank had just closed on one of the largest ever international joint ventures with a financial consortium in Europe and another banking group in Latin America. This far-reaching partnership was the centerpiece of the groundbreaking strategy the Blue Pod had proposed months earlier.

Above the clamor, Jack held up his glass and bellowed a toast. "Alright kids, let's all drink to the success of the Joval Financial Group! To Joval!" Everyone echoed the toast, raised their glasses and drank.

Lee leaned over to Adam privately and said, "Here's the difference I see between Jack and Manny. With Jack, we're all students and he's the teacher. With Manny, we're the faculty and he's the principal." Adam nodded in agreement.

Principal Manny was on the side of the room, chatting with managers from other pods. He was biding his time, waiting for the moment. Jack was in rare form as he conversed with a group of partners about what the *Financial Times* had written about Joval's bold move in such an uncertain economy. He was energetic and loud. He would periodically slap the back of whoever was in range when he made a point or thought it was time for them to laugh. The white wine he was drinking must have been quite flavorful. It was only an hour into the party and he was working on his fifth glass.

Manny excused himself and walked across the room slowly, making eye contact with Linda who joined him. He motioned to Lee, and soon Lee too was navigating through the crowd in Jack's direction. Rachel was in another corner, watching everything. She didn't know what was going on but she knew enough to know she couldn't afford to miss the action. She ordered another screwdriver and found a nice couch within earshot.

She sat down. Her perfect view became partially obstructed by a woman with big hair, a tight please-look-at-me dress and far too much makeup. A swath of shiny red lipstick exaggerated the pout of collagen-inflated lips. She was the kind of person you'd sooner see in Miami or L.A. than in New York. Some consultant's guest, Rachel assumed.

Jack stood with three other partners and Deborah Hopkins in a circle of power. Deborah made some remarks about how Joval's high profile publicity would now help attract more clients to Cyrus & Hopkins. She raised her glass and was making a toast "to publicity" when Manny, Lee and Linda joined the periphery of the group. They raised their glasses as well. Deborah asked Lee, "Did you ever imagine when you started this project that it would end up having such a significant worldwide impact?"

Lee of course confessed that no one could have known. He entertained the crowd with tidbits about the different phases of research, Manny's skilled handling of the team, and Linda's crowning strategy. Jack was beaming in his glory as he slapped Lee on the back with his free hand.

At that point, Linda took it upon herself to bestow upon the group more details about the Boston meeting. She then mentioned that working on the assignment had only heightened her interest in working on another high profile case like the one Manny was pursuing.

All eyes flew to Manny. Jack took a sip of wine.

"Nothing is for sure," Manny said. "It's just a lead with Osanto's Bar & Grill that may not work out in the end."

"Well, where do things stand now? Are they interested in us?" asked Ira Davidson, a partner with the Red Pod.

Manny responded, "Well, they're somewhat interested, but it may not be worth our time. It seems they want us to do a small introductory assignment before they seriously consider us for the nationwide deal with their parent company."

Jack jumped in. "The initial project is really beneath our range and the guy Manny spoke to can't guarantee that we'll get to work on the bigger deal." He raised his glass again. "Anyhow, this is a day to celebrate our huge Joval success. If we're not too greedy, and don't waste our resources, we'll come out of this recession strong and steadfast. We have plenty of work do to. I wouldn't want to distract and disappoint our associates by leading them on a chase after the wind."

The only wind that Manny could discern was streaming out of Jack's mouth.

Deborah and the other partners quickly turned back to Manny. It was like a pro tennis match; the spectator's heads were synchronized to follow the ball wherever it dashed. Manny could tell that Deborah smelled money. He scratched his chin and offered, "Perhaps there's a way to keep our foot in the door without taking the pod away from their work." He shook his head. "Eh, never mind."

Deborah scrambled into action so fast she spilled some of her martini on the floor. "No, wait! What's your idea?"

Manny worked hard to suppress a smile. Seeing Linda's discrete grin didn't help him either. He made sure to speak to Jack directly. "What if we offered your students an opportunity to do extra homework for extra credit? What if we asked if anyone would be willing to take on the Osanto project in addition to their normal workload? We could reward them with a larger-than-usual bonus—perhaps a percentage of the proceeds from the national project, should we get it."

The tennis ball had been returned and the spectators followed dutifully. As his fellow partners stared at him, Jack could see ambitions circling around in their heads, like sharks in an aquarium tank ready for an underwater gate to be opened. If Jack wouldn't devour the opportunity, the other partners gladly would.

Jack said, "Very well. Find your volunteers." So casual. He might as well have said, I'll have fries with that.

Could it have been that easy? Evidently so. Jack raised his glass again, which had been filled again by a roving waiter, and said, "Here's to Osanto's, our extra credit project for the semester."

"Here, here!" said Deborah and they all drank. "I have a feeling this will all work out fine. Time is of the essence, though. Jack, shouldn't he get started right away?"

"You should get started right away," said Jack.

Manny thanked Jack and walked away. Lee followed a minute after and caught up with Manny. "That was epic!" Manny exclaimed, dripping with delight. "Would you do your best to encourage as many associates as possible to volunteer? The more people we have, the fewer hours we'll each have to work."

Lee's heart danced with visions of an adventure to come. "Say no more. I'll round up the troops." Lee was turning out to be quite a dependable ally.

Once the *Deborah, Jack & Manny Show* was over, the meatballs enticed Rachel back to the buffet table for seconds. She reached to grab the last meatball, when another pair of tongs snatched it away at the last second. She looked up to find the makeup woman on the opposite side of the table, holding the elusive meatball and exclaiming, "I can't believe I'm here. What a wonderful party tonight."

Rachel sighed with an obligatory, "Yes, quite wonderful."

"I'm so impressed with everyone at this firm."

"Yes, it's quite a place to work at."

The woman scanned the room. "Some of the top minds in business are in this crowd. I don't know why I haven't been able to have a serious discussion so far."

Rachel said, "Sweetie, I'm sure it has nothing to do with your makeup."

❖   ❖   ❖

CHAPTER TEN

Monday morning couldn't arrive fast enough for the Blue Pod associates. They couldn't wait to see what would happen next with the Osanto's project. Who would volunteer for this experiment?

Linda picked up her computer and proceeded to Manny's office. It was time for the next installment of their discussion on Life and leadership. Manny was on the phone but motioned for her to come in and take a seat.

"Alright, Jack. No problem. Bye." Manny hung up.

Linda decided it wasn't too nosy to inquire, "Did he bite your head off after the party on Friday?"

"No." Manny looked surprised. "He seems fine. I'm not sure what he's thinking, but he's treating me like he normally does."

"Which still leaves room for improvement."

Manny smiled in response. He had been trying to prevent his associates from being dragged into the quagmire of his relationship problems with Jack, but apparently everyone could tell what was going on.

They headed for the discussion area and Manny asked, "This time, would you mind starting off? I'd love to learn from you as well. Tell me what's important to you about leadership. It could be something we've covered so far or something new."

"Okay." Linda was a little taken aback, but not that much. Manny was known for turning the tables on associates, but always in the service of building them up. "I guess I'll start off with a leadership attribute that I see in you. You don't look out for yourself as much as you look out for our assignment or the pod. I've always believed that once you become a leader, it's not about your personal glory anymore. A good leader should know that her individual success means nothing. A leader's glory radiates from the success of her group."

"That's beautiful and so true," Manny exclaimed. "Most people don't comprehend that a promotion to a leadership position isn't just a promotion. It should be a conversion. No longer are you an individual contributor, but now you're supposed to be a new person, a leader. From now on you'll be judged by the work that takes place on *other* people's desks."

Linda offered, "I think it's a difficult conversion for most people because it goes against the way we've learned how to win. Ever since our first jobs and even as far back as elementary school, we were taught that the way to win is to stand out in a crowd. But the way to win changes when you're a leader. A leader wins when her team stands out."

Manny nodded his head. "Linda, I want you to know that you're a good leader to the others in the pod, and I'm not only talking about when you facilitate pod meetings. You don't need a position or title to be a leader, you just need Life." He looked her in the eyes. "You're going to become a very powerful leader one day."

A look of doubt flooded Linda's face. "Manny, I heard Jennifer Wynn's leaving. Do you think I should throw my hat in the ring for her position?" Jennifer was the manager of the Green Pod. She had announced her upcoming departure from the firm in order to work for a consumer packaged goods company. None of the associates in the Green Pod were being seriously considered to take her place, or at least that's what the grapevine had to say. This meant that the Hiring and Promotions Committee would have to find replacement candidates from another pod or outside the firm.

Manny waited long enough for her to know that he meant his response. "I know you'll make a great manager. Go for the position."

She still had a reluctant look about her. "Frankly, I don't want to get my hand slapped again. You know, I was turned down for a manager's position last year. Then there was your position I didn't get this year. So this would be the third time. I'm not sure yet if it's worth it for me to apply."

Manny held his chin in the palm of his hand. "Tell me why you want the position."

"Last year, honestly, I applied because it seemed like it was the next logical achievement in my career. Then, this year I applied for your position because I was curious about what it's like to lead. But now I want to lead because I want to make Life happen. You know, the way you do."

"Linda, that's the best reason of all. I know you'd bring a lot of Life to all your associates. You'd get some real results from them too. So, since your competence isn't in question, the only thing left to ask is simply: how fiercely do you want it?"

She paused and thought. "I want it badly. I just don't know if I'll ever be able to do what you do, Manny. I'm not an extrovert like you. I get tired of having to deal with people all day long at work. I often find Life from being alone, just curling up with a good book in front of a fireplace. If I want to be a good leader, this may be a problem."

"No problem," Manny replied. "I'm an extrovert and you're an introvert. But neither one of us has a monopoly on what it takes to be a leader. Leading well has little to do with your personality, but has everything to do with your behavior. If your behavior leads your people to Life, you're a good leader. It takes all kinds of leaders to make an organization robust and resilient. Some of my favorite leaders on the planet are introverts! It doesn't matter that your style is more reserved than mine; all that matters is that you continue to be broken in."

Linda felt hope swelling within her. In her mind, she revoked the rule she had made up that she couldn't be a skillful leader. Her personality would do just fine. Her natural curiosity was back in action. "You keep on talking about being broken in as a leader, but what does being broken in mean to you?"

"At last, the million-dollar question. When I say that a leader is being broken in, I'm talking about a process that trains the leader how to make Life happen at a greatly accelerated pace compared to most people. It has nothing to do with being broken or damaged. It's the same idea as the breaking-in process that gives a new pair of dress shoes a better fit. New shoes need training to become comfortable. Likewise, a baseball glove doesn't work best when it's stiff and brand new. When you get a new glove, you spend a long time trying to break it in so that it works better, so it finally 'fits like a glove.' In the same way, a leader can create powerful results through human assistants once he's been broken in by Life.

"All leaders grow older but not all of us grow wiser. Wisdom is a choice. There's a cost involved in choosing to grow wiser in the ways of Life. Every college student has to invest time, money and effort in order to learn academically. Well, we too have to invest time and energy in order to become effective as leaders. We have to be broken in. Today I want to talk today about the goal of the breaking-in process. The next time we talk, I'll give you the details of the breaking-in process itself. Does that sound okay to you?"

"Sure." She nodded.

"The last time we talked, I hinted that there's a way to make Life multiply exponentially in other people. It's a way of doing Life that's unique to people of true influence."

"Yes. How could I forget your cliffhanger of an ending? You told me that it involves blending two personal traits into one."

"That's right. I'm about to reveal the secret blend, and frankly, you may or may not appreciate it at first, so let it percolate in your mind. The two traits that must be blended are confidence and humility. A broken-in leader is a master at mixing powerful confidence and deep humility to make Life happen. When a leader demonstrates these strong and gentle traits together, she then has her strength under control and Life explodes among followers at an accelerated pace. The results are powerful.

"We've all heard of powerful leaders who've grabbed the attention and co-operation of the masses with so-called virtues of steel. You know, politicians and executives who strong-armed people into complying with their agenda. But that's not the way it was with the great leaders in history like Nelson Mandela, Mother Theresa, Martin Luther King, Jr., Mahatma Gandhi, Abraham Lincoln, Cyrus the Great, and King David, just to name a few."

"An inspiring group, to say the least."

"Indeed. These were broken-in leaders. They were strong-willed and modest. They blended steel and velvet virtues together and succeeded in capturing far more than people's compliance; they secured their followers' devotion. They also secured the superior results that flow only from devotion. They unleashed such initiative and resolve in their people that they birthed movements. How's that for getting results? What I'm talking about isn't some new fad in leadership; it's ancient. The greatest men and women throughout human history have modeled it. They may not have used my exact words to describe their styles, but my words point to a truth that was present in their leadership in a crystal clear way. They kept their strength under control to make Life show up in their people and their missions." Manny wondered if

Linda was tracking with him. He could tell it was a new way of thinking for her.

"Alright," she uttered, inviting Manny to say more.

"Confidence and humility are the only sure way to make Life happen. Now, when I say confidence, I'm not just referring to self-confidence. I'm referring to a whole spectrum of strong qualities that a confident person possesses, like courage, tenacity, boldness, determination and inner resolve."

"Is there a spectrum of humble qualities too?"

"Yes. Humility involves traits like personal sacrifice, consideration of others, self-control, modesty, co-operation and integrity. Integrity is a humble trait because it takes great humility to override your emotions and choose to do what's right when every bone in your body wants to go another way."

"Most people take for granted that you need to possess the confident qualities if you want to lead," Linda added.

"And it's true, since leading is not for wimps. Everybody knows that. But few people stop and consider that the raw power of a leader has to be filtered so that it only brings out the best in people. Humility is the filter. It ensures that a leader's display of strength is used only in the Life-giving ways that inspire people to produce real results. We want confident leaders, not arrogant leaders. The difference between confidence and arrogance is humility. The filter of humility is the reason why a leader's strengths make people come alive at work. Without confident humility, the leader is just your average selfish, arrogant boss. That kind of boldness only turns people off."

"I get it." New bullet points populated Linda's document. She added a thought or two of her own as well:

- **When you're promoted from an individual contributor to a leader, a conversion has to happen in your thinking: although you've**

**always learned to win by personally stand-
ing out, now the way to win is to make your
team's performance stand out.**

- **People spend a long time trying to break in
a new baseball glove so that it works better.
In the same way, a leader must be broken in
to sustainably create powerful results
through human assistants. The breaking-in
process is designed to impart confident
humility (steel and velvet) into a leader so
she can make Life happen.**

- **Compelling leaders blend steel and velvet
virtues to secure the superior team results
that only come from devotion. What devotion? The followers' devotion to their mission, to each other and to their leader.**

- **Some of the best leaders are introverts. It
doesn't matter if your style is introverted or
extroverted (Life requires all types of leaders). The only thing that matters is that your
leadership style has been broken in with
confident humility.**

A thought hit Linda. "Is this blended trait a best practice you
brought to work from home?"

"Absolutely. I used to notice how much Life flowed freely
through my family but how rare it was in my company. I asked
myself, 'What's the difference that causes Life to flow in one
organization but not the other?' And this blended trait appeared
to be the decisive factor. Let's use an example from home.
Actually, Linda, why don't you provide one? Tell me about a time
when your mom provided Life for you."

"Okay. Mama sacrificed her dream of going back to school
and becoming a nurse just so my sister and I could go to college.

She worked at two jobs to make sure we had the education we needed."

Manny nodded his head. "You see, she showed both self restraint, a humble trait, and tenacity, a confident trait, when she put her own dream on the back burner and fought for her daughters' dreams. That was your mother's confident humility in action. When you practice confident humility, you refuse to let anything stop you from connecting your followers with the Life they need."

"Mama's always been my hero. And I see what you're saying. She led in a very confident way, but she was humble too."

"You get the chance to practice a lot of confident humility as a parent. I'll use an example from my own family. I'm one of those people who needs their sleep. Once I'm down, it's very frustrating for me to wake up unless I have seven or eight hours of sleep behind me. When Ryan was about three years old, he went through a stage where he would routinely come to my bedside and tap me on the shoulder around 4 a.m. because he was scared of the dark. I'd be startled and wake up with bleary eyes and my heart thumping. And I'm too ashamed to say out loud the thoughts that would run through my head when I was jolted out of a sound sleep. Amazingly, Ryan still lives! And why did I indulge him night after night by getting out of bed to show him that there was no monster in the corner? Because being a dad requires lots of humility and resolve. That same kind of confident humility is what makes your people thrive at work too. Anything less causes dysfunction in followers. Confident humility is the key to protecting and advancing the Life of your team. It's what separates those who lead from those who pretend to lead."

"Impressive."

Manny smiled.

"I can see why you called confident humility a way of Life," Linda said. "As I reflect on my mother, she wasn't always perfectly confident or humble, but she was always trying to be good at it. Her confident humility wasn't a one-time decision. She had to practice it every day to make Life happen for her family."

"Linda," Manny was hesitant to speak. "I don't always get humility right and I'm not always as confident as I need to be, but I can't stop trying. And as I've been practicing confident humility over the last months, I've been seeing signs of Life in the Blue Pod. Everyone's producing more, getting along better, having fun—I can't tell you how overjoyed I am."

"Wait a minute." Linda got up. She paced the floor without saying anything more. Manny was naturally curious to know what she was thinking. She took a while walking back and forth. Finally, Manny stood up too. It was less awkward that way.

She broke the silence with a question that sounded like a statement. "The pieces of the puzzle are coming together now, aren't they? When we were in Boston, you know, the Boston surprise, you were practicing confident humility to make Life happen for me. You sacrificed your time in front of Deborah so I could shine, and it happened: I felt a surge of Life. I was thriving like never before. I was doing what I was born to do. I experienced a sense of connection and adventure and purpose that was bigger than me." She looked at him with piercing eyes.

Manny sat down, blushing slightly.

She spoke slowly, signaling the finding of the words as she said them. "You said you *wanted* to sacrifice for me. It must have taken a lot of inner strength to be that humble considering that I seemed more like an enemy than a friend at that time." She laughed. "I was barely on speaking terms with you because I felt like you had stolen my position."

He tapped his hand against the side of his pants and chuckled briefly. She started pacing again. "But was it an unthinking act or was it on purpose? I mean, were you intentionally being confident and humble so I could have Life?"

"Yes." He was staring at the floor when he responded.

"Manny."

He looked up and met her eyes.

"Thank you," she said simply with a smile.

Manny was deeply touched by her gratitude. It would have been enough had she thanked him for the most superficial layer of his sacrifice, but instead she saw all the way through to his core motivation. Like Susan and Noah before her, Linda had acknowledged him as one who paid the price to convey Life.

PART FOUR

❖   ❖   ❖

The Expedition

❖   ❖   ❖

CHAPTER ELEVEN

L ight streamed through the upper windows of the
     concourse, painting intricate murals of shadow and
     brightness on the vast floor below. The space inside
Grand Central Station carried a serene and sacred air about it
even though multitudes of commuters were milling about.
The masses were still half asleep. Their quiet grace was
characteristic of the early morning commute.

The pre-determined meeting point was the central
information booth with the clock on top. Manny stood next
to the booth with a bottle of water and his bag slung over his
shoulder. He wore a trench coat over his suit. A little more
than a week had passed since his showdown with Jack at the
cocktail party.

Manny checked his watch again (6:03 a.m.) and searched
the immense hall for familiar faces. Nope. He'd issued the
invitation very casually during one of the pod meetings the
week prior. "If anyone wants to volunteer for the Osanto's
assignment in addition to your other projects, just meet me
by the clock booth in Grand Central at 6:15 on Monday
morning." The plan was for the volunteers and him to catch
the 6:48 train to Stamford to meet Osanto's management.

Manny now questioned the wisdom of requesting the associates to just show up. No "email me." No "raise your hand if you're interested." Just "meet me at dawn." Too dramatic, he reflected, like a line from some B movie.

But how many associates would show up. Two? Four? Would there be enough to get the project done in a respectable timeframe for the client? Or would he be alone, staying up all night long for weeks on end? Did the associates like him and the project enough to volunteer for this?

Certainly Jack wouldn't be coming. He would be out of town for the week chasing new clients at some conference in Florida. At any rate, Jack had made it clear: "This is *your* extra-credit assignment." Read: don't ask me for help, Manny. And Manny was fine with Jack's hands-off policy. No more waiting for Jack's grudging approval every step of the way. Finally, here was a project all his own. It was time to spread his wings.

The first associate to step into the shadow of his wings was Tom Walker. "Glad you could make it," Manny said, shaking the hand of the half-comatose consultant who had a large band-aid stretched over his chin. "What happened to you?"

"Never attempt to shave with a blade before five in the morning," he stammered out in his sleepiness.

"Wise." Manny shook his head. "So very wise."

Next came Linda. A few minutes later Lee and Adam emerged from the masses, both walking at a snail's pace with their heads down as they typed their text messages. A small sound of delight squeaked out of Manny's mouth when he saw them coming. Unbelievably, by 6:14, all eight of the Blue Pod's associates had arrived. Every single associate had volunteered! Manny worked to keep his elation in check, but he couldn't stop smiling. No one accidentally volunteers by getting up at 4:30 in the morning!

The first order of business was to head downstairs for coffee in the food court. A homeless man with plenty of tattoos and body odor was sitting a few feet from the bottom of the escalator, extending a paper coffee cup. He shook the cup every few seconds, rattling the change inside. The associates filed past him one by one. Manny, the last one off the escalator, walked past him too. After a few seconds, Manny slowed down, made an about-face and went back to the man. The associates continued ahead in their sleepwalk toward caffeine.

The man looked up to meet Manny's golden eyes. Manny looked as if he were deciding something. "I don't usually give change. I give money to a homeless shelter in the Bowery instead." The man remained silent. "But I have a feeling about you." Manny pulled two dollars from his wallet, crouched down, and put them in the cup. "Please make sure you buy food with this." The man smiled.

At the coffee stand, Lee was the first to realize Manny's absence. He turned around and scanned the food court. He was surprised to see Manny touching the elbow of the homeless man and then getting up and walking towards the pod.

Minutes later, the group boarded the silver and red Metro North commuter train sitting on track 111. The car they chose had plenty of empty seats even though it was rush hour; northbound travel at that time wasn't so bad since the suburban residents competed mostly for southbound seats.

The pod members sat near each other. The train jolted into movement and started its journey through the dark tunnel. Manny looked around. These were good people, he affirmed to himself as he whipped out a pad of paper. He wrote out his double list, just as he did every Monday: the first list contained his to-do items for the workweek, and the second had the same items placed in the order which would make the pod and his clients thrive the most. If I don't get to the things on the bottom of the list this week, that's okay, he thought.

As the train emerged into daylight, some of the associates were observing the status of Manny's head with interest. Adam had a prime view since he was sitting directly behind Manny. The head started a long, gradual arc to the left until it was jerked back to equilibrium. Next, it commenced a slow drift to the right—no, no, no, back to the left. Yes, more, more and a little bit more. His head finally came to rest on the window. He was out. Adam exhaled. All were now exempt from having to use the train ride as a planning session for the day ahead. So one by one, everyone else fell asleep on the ride to Connecticut.

"Be careful," Manny cautioned as they stepped onto the breezy platform at Stamford. "Richard's given us carte blanche to do what we need, but we have to partner with his internal task force. It's a multidisciplinary group with about half of them coming from the Marketing Department. They may not be as eager as Richard to have outside help so let's remember to be sensitive. We don't want them to view us as competition. Whatever you do, don't keep any vital information to yourselves. Share everything you've got with the task force. We're supposed to be collaborating with them on this, and I'm certain Richard will be asking them for their opinion as to whether we should get the big national contract."

The team poured itself into three taxis waiting outside the station. Manny, Adam and Linda packed themselves like sardines into the back of one of the cabs. They rode through downtown Stamford and onto a highway that carried them through some wooded areas. They were quietly taking in the scenery when out of the blue Manny turned to Adam with, "I was discussing leadership with Linda the other day and I told her that leaders have to embrace humility to be effective. Do you agree with that?"

Adam was smiling on the inside because Manny had become famous for impromptu, brain-depleting chats. This was the first time that a random chat had been initiated so dangerously early in the morning though. Adam gave in. "I've never thought about it that way." He considered the notion, scratching his beard as if to validate the process. "Yeah, I agree. Leaders can't just act in their own interests all the time, so they've gotta be humble."

"What does being humble mean to you?"

"I guess being submissive for a greater purpose."

"Interesting." His eyes turned next to Linda, "And what does it mean to you?"

She had to think for a minute too, but finally came up with, "I think it's about being modest and assisting others."

A moment passed and although no one said anything new, Manny blurted out, "What's that? What's my definition? Well I'm glad you asked. My definition is different." Adam and Linda flashed each other a look of mock misery as if to say, we definitely should have taken another cab.

Manny continued without skipping a beat. "I think true humility has to come from strength. I'm not a big fan of humility that flows from insecurity and personal weakness. You can't lead from insecurity, otherwise people will walk all over you. You need to be strong and have your strength under the control of humility. To me, confident humility is the state of being so comfortable with yourself that no selfless task is beneath you. It means doing the hard work of learning how valuable you really are, until you reach the point that you no longer have to use your actions to prove you're important. You know you can't lose. You're grounded enough to do whatever the mission requires, important-looking or not."

Linda piped up, "Example please."

"Okay." He cocked his head to the side. "I was watching the news the other night and they showed an archived video clip of Princess Diana visiting an orphanage in a developing country. The little child she was holding in her arms accidentally dropped a toy or something. The princess crouched down to the floor, picked up the toy and gave it back to the child. Now, are either of you tempted to think less of the princess for stooping to the floor and helping? After all, she was performing a menial task for a so-called 'nobody.'"

"Of course not," Adam returned.

"And do you think Princess Diana wasted even a second worrying that people might confuse her for a nanny or a janitor?" Manny answered his own question, "Of course not. She knew she was a princess and everyone else did too. Since she had nothing left to prove, she could humbly perform the selfless task without fear of how it looked. That's the way we should be. That's why we should focus night and day on learning how essential we truly are."

"But isn't that sort of prideful?" Linda volunteered.

"It's not prideful or selfish because when you have nothing left to prove to yourself, then you can afford to invest in the person in front of you without reservations. That's how you graduate from being one of those terminally boring leaders who look out for themselves all the time."

Linda mulled things over. "Why is it so hard for us to believe that we really count? We spend so much time trying to be admired or respected or even feared by other people. What we're really doing is trying to prove to ourselves that we're special." Then a different look came across Linda's face. "You know, sometimes it's hard for me to honor other people's interests over my own because it makes me feel less worthy. It makes me feel like maybe they deserve good things more than I do because I'm not that important."

Manny replied, "I know what you're talking about. I lived out of that mindset for a long time, but I discovered that that way of thinking is actually false humility. It's a stumbling block to the confident type of humility that makes the world go around. I've heard it said that being humble doesn't mean thinking less of yourself, it simply means thinking of yourself less. It's never okay to invest in others because you believe you're worth less than they are. That's not real humility; that's an inner defect in your thinking that has to be overcome. True humility comes from inner strength. It's knowing how powerfully important you are, to the point that no selfless action you take ever poses a threat to your self-image."

Adam asked, "But can't growing your self-worth make you arrogant too? What about all those prideful leaders who think they're important and treat everyone else like hell?"

"Great question. Yeah, focusing on your worth can lead to an oversized ego, but only if you start believing one of two lies in the process. So long as you stick with the truth, then you'll only grow more humble as you grow in self-worth."

Adam asked the obvious question. "And the two lies are…?"

"First, believing you're not important, and second, believing you're more important than everyone else. In the case of the first lie, the leader acts like he knows that he's important when he doesn't know it yet *intuitively*. In his head, the misguided leader says to himself, 'I'm important.' But his emotions still scream 'I'm inferior and unworthy to be a leader.' His intuition will often speak louder than his intellect, so he'll try to drown out the fearful voices by acting 'important' and enforcing the do-it-or-else approach to leadership. The lie he believes is that intellectual knowledge of his self-worth is sufficient for him to lead well. But to be an effective leader, he needs complete knowledge—head and heart knowledge—of his worth. Otherwise he'll end up dominating people and never truly listening to others, all to prove to his doubting heart that he's really important. Whenever you find him being pushy, he's really just trying to achieve the temporary high of feeling 'in charge' and therefore important. He's trying to prove his importance to his doubting heart whether he realizes it or not."

Linda leaned forward and placed her hand on the back of the front seat. "I had that kind of boss at the investment bank where I used to work. There was a civil war raging between his intellect and his emotions. All the people who reported to him got caught in the crossfire."

Manny nodded in agreement. "In the second case, the leader's head and heart may both agree that he's important, but arrogance makes him ineffective as a leader because he's living out a different lie: that he's more important than the other human beings who work for him. That's crazy. The only thing a leader possesses that's superior is the authority given to him to orchestrate work. He's not superior in worth. What the heck does some bureaucratic authority have to do with the value of a human Life? We all spring from the same human family. Isn't it amazing how the brothers and sisters in a typical family can grow up to be so different? Some may become leaders and others may not. But a good parent would never make the mistake of thinking that one child is inherently more valuable than another. All the members are exceedingly valuable."

"So how does a leader move beyond those lies?" asked Adam.

"Well, in the first place, a leader has to want to grow beyond the lie he believes. If he does, then he needs to do some thinking and come up with a better way to embrace his worth. The first type of leader has to find a way to move the knowledge of his worth from his head to his heart. The second type needs to discover that others are just as important as he is. These discoveries take time. It's hard for people to become honest with themselves and to redefine their self-worth. That's why every leader needs the help of a friend. Not just any friend—a humble and fearless friend who can support them over an extended period of time. Someone who can be brutally honest. That someone might be a friend or a mentor, but it may also be an executive coach or a counselor."

Linda was smiling as she looked at the trees over on her side of the car. She was familiar with the fact that Manny could dispense wisdom at the drop of a hat. Adam, on the other hand, was silent the way one is quiet when one stumbles onto something essential without knowing why.

Manny turned to Adam. "I've been noticing your interactions with people over the last months. You've been learning to put other associates first. I even heard that you stayed late on Friday to help Tom with his work. Sounds like you're learning how to rest in the fact that you're immensely valuable. Keep up the good work. Keep on pursuing the knowledge of your worth with confidence and humility, and you'll soon find yourself becoming quite a leader. People will definitely follow your lead."

Adam sat in silence, taking it all in, not knowing what to say. It never occurred to him that someone could observe his inmost efforts to believe the best of himself. Even Adam hadn't noticed his own progress, but now he couldn't deny the truth of the gradual change that had been happening from the inside out. It felt somewhat odd to be so... seen, but it was comforting. Adam began to recognize that Manny's humility at work had made a space for Adam's self-worth and confidence to grow. Looking out the window, Adam mentioned, "You remind me of my high school football coach."

Linda scribbled some shorthand notes onto a pad she had in her bag:

- **A broken-in leader makes Life happen by demonstrating confidence and humility. But humility is a far more compelling concept than most people realize.**
- **Humility is the state of being so comfortable with yourself that no selfless task is beneath you. Do the hard work of learning how valuable you really are until you don't have to use your activities to prove your importance. You're on the right track when your emotions start to grasp that you have nothing to lose by taking humble actions. That's how you know you're a well-grounded person.**
- **Humility doesn't mean thinking less of yourself; it means thinking of yourself less often**

because you're already in touch with your immeasurable worth.

- Increasing your understanding of your self-worth is not selfish; it's actually the most secure basis for serving others selflessly. Don't avoid growing your self-worth because you're afraid you'll grow arrogant (that's false humility). You'll be fine as long as you (1) seek to know your great worth at the heart level as well as intellectually; and (2) increase your understanding of other people's worth as well as your own.

- When you have nothing left to prove, you can afford to invest in the person in front of you rather than watching out for yourself all the time (which is so boring).

- Life requires leaders to rely on vast reserves of accurate self-worth. Pursuing this heart-level experience is a journey. We're not designed to make the journey alone. Surround yourself with fearless, humble, Life-filled mentors and friends who can help you see yourself as you truly are. Also, using a Life coach, a pastor or a counselor may be a good idea.

The long driveway weaved through the fields of grass and delivered the pod to the headquarters of Osanto's Bar & Grill, Inc. The property had a cluster of three identical low-rise office buildings made of blond concrete and turquoise glass. A small neon "Osanto's" logo adorned the upper right hand corner of building closest to the highway.

The group climbed out of the convoy and sat down in the deep armchairs of the lobby. Manny went upstairs to meet with Richard. Within twenty minutes, the associates had been escorted into a third-floor conference room with Manny, Richard and the members of the internal task force. They were surrounded by botanical prints on the walls and a couple of porcelain figurines. The view through the windows was of the grassy grounds and the parking lot with some trees in the distance.

Richard was a rotund man with a balding head and a cherubic face. He spoke in a sing-songy way that was entertaining at best, distracting at worst. The members of the task force called him Ricky. He wore a green polo shirt and jeans. Everyone at Osanto's was wearing casual clothes, making the suit-clad associates feel entirely overdressed. While Richard introduced the members of the task force, the associates discretely slipped off their jackets and ties. Manny discretely slipped a note down his side of the table that read: "Sorry. Completely forgot to ask about attire."

Richard, who now insisted the pod also call him Ricky, warned the group that the idea of changing Osanto's menu was highly confidential. He wanted only a handful of people in his organization to know about it in case the proposed changes didn't pan out. "A change of menu could have far-reaching implications for how we choose our food suppliers, how the training department instructs chefs, and even the strategy behind our advertising. I don't want my folks rearranging their departments needlessly. "

The associates were instructed to only call their engagement "Project X" and to be especially careful not to mention details to any employees who were not on the Project X task force. If any Osanto's employees other than the task force members asked why the consultants were on site, the associates were to say they were simply conducting some market research for Ricky and leave it at that.

"We've historically been a very profitable company. However, as you'll see in the reports in front of you, our overall revenues reached a plateau and recently began trending somewhat downward." Ricky had a slightly embarrassed look on his face, but it went as quickly as it came. "Anyway, the corporate management team and I were toying with new ways to expand our customer base without upsetting our current customers by changing the menu too much. That's when the trans-fat ban was passed in New York. It threw us all for a loop. We realized that if changes had to be made to our menu, we might as well do it right and change the smart way. That's where you guys come in. Your market experience will hopefully help us make the right choices. In the next few months we want a healthier menu. We want to be trans-fat free *and* we want to expand our customer base *and* we don't want to alienate our existing customers."

The facts were these: four kinds of fats are found in foods. Health experts had dubbed monounsaturated and polyunsaturated fats the "good" fats. It was also known that adults should eat far less saturated fats. And more recently, the world was discovering that the last kind of fat, trans fat, was the absolute worst of the four. Researchers found that even small daily amounts of this artificially created fat were connected to heart disease.

Noting that heart disease had caused many deaths in New York City, the city's Board of Health voted to ban restaurants from using trans fats in their food.

So Ricky's challenge to the Project X Task Force was twofold: first, they would find a way to ensure that their old dishes tasted the same way, even while using a new substitute for trans fats. Second, they were to identify a way to attract new, health-oriented customers without offending the old customers.

Ricky sang on about the way he wanted the research done and the timelines involved. Adam studied the faces of the task force members sitting across the table. He wondered the same thing the whole Blue Pod was wondering: would the Project X Task Force make this an easy or difficult experience for the pod?

CHAPTER TWELVE

Manny was back at the offices of Cyrus & Hopkins on Tuesday. There was a bounce in his step as he strolled down the hallway. He was singing an eighties song when he walked in his office.

Rachel was next to his desk, placing some mail in his inbox. "Who's the guy who sang that song?" she asked.

"Thomas Dolby."

"Yes. Let's leave it that way," she said with a smile.

Rachel walked out as Linda walked in, humming a tune as well. Rachel turned around in time to catch Manny asking Linda, "Who used to sing that?" Rachel and Manny burst into laughter.

Linda was less amused. "I guess you had to be there."

On account of the spring-like weather, Manny and Linda decided to have their chat outside on the twenty-seventh floor terrace. They had their choice of seats since it was mid-morning and still too early for the first round of coffee-breakers to appear. They steered over to some chairs overlooking Manhattan's West Side. You could see past the Hudson River and halfway across New Jersey on a clear day, though that particular day was hazy.

Linda settled in. "All I can think about is that Green Pod position. Your little pep talk inspired me, so I threw my hat in the ring. I have the interviews scheduled for this afternoon."

"So I've heard," Manny responded. He felt a tinge of sadness. He genuinely wanted to see Linda promoted but it hadn't sunk in until now that she could well be leaving the pod. "I'll do everything in my power to support you, Linda. I'll start by sending a recommendation letter to the Hiring and Promotions Committee. You're going to make a great manager. And I've seen you hanging out with some of the Greenies before—they like you already."

"I hope so. This promotion means a lot to me. I've been waiting for a long, long time for leadership responsibility. I want to make the pod thrive."

"I know you will. By the way, I heard that Bernadette Waters has also applied for the position." Bernadette was a lanky, red-haired consultant who coincidentally came from the Red Pod. Technology was her specialty. She often traveled to IT conferences and networked with CIO's and the like. "I don't know her super-well, but for whatever it's worth, I think you'd probably do a better job leading than she would. You're a great leader."

"Thanks. We'll see how things go. I may also have to deal with some resistance from Jack. He made it clear that he likes having my skill set around for the Blue Pod."

"Don't worry about Jack. I'll handle him if necessary." Manny then pulled a wad of folded papers out of the bag he'd brought with him. "Would you believe I actually did some homework for today? I got together with my friend Noah this weekend. He's a great leader who knows a lot about the ways of Life. Anyhow, Susan, Noah and I created a rough framework to clarify the breaking-in process of a leader." He shuffled through the papers. "We printed out a copy for you." He gave Linda a page.

Linda was about to read it but she waited a moment so Manny could finish his thoughts. He was excited. "The core of being a good leader is intentionally having your strength under control in a way that generates Life. What separates broken-in leaders from all other leaders is that they intentionally choose to make Life happen for others in this confident and humble way. The breaking-in process is what drives confidence and humility deep into a leader's heart and enables her to unleash Life in her followers at an accelerated pace."

Manny pulled out his own copy of the page and stuck the rest of the papers back into his bag. "You know, before this weekend with Susan and Noah, I never stopped to articulate the steps I go through when I'm leading. It all just seemed like one big process. But when we discussed it, we agreed that there were three separate steps that should happen every time you make a leadership decision. So here's the flow of things." He read the text off the page:

The Breaking-In Process of a Leader (How to make daily decisions)

  1. Discover how Life wants to show up right now.

  2. Invent an action plan to make that Life happen.

  3. Execute the plan with confident humility.

Then learn from your success and mistakes, go back to step one, and do it again.

"A leader makes dozens of everyday decisions and we have lots of tools in the toolbox to choose from. Should I resolve this conflict for my people or let them work it out? What strategy should I pursue to increase productivity? Whenever you have to make a decision as a leader, the first thing to do is to stop the world long enough to discover how Life wants to show up. For instance, when I started with the firm, it didn't seem as if you were even close to thriving. So I took the first step by figuring out where your Life was likely to come from. Since you had recently been passed over for the promotion you wanted, I suspected that Life would show up if you got a shot at some greater responsibility and recognition. So that was how I did step one, discovering how Life wants to show up. Do you want to take a guess as to how I did step two?"

Linda was more than used to Manny's give-and-take conversational style by now, so she was ready to roll. "Let's see." She read from the paper, "Step two. Invent an action plan to make that Life happen." She paused, then said, "I guess once you figured out that the most Life would come from giving me responsibility, you then thought up the required action step to make it happen, which was giving me the opportunity to present."

"Absolutely. I came up with several steps I could potentially take but—and this is important—the special way I came up with them was quite intentional. I first made up my mind to make Life happen for you even if the action steps came at my personal expense. I chose not to consider it too much of an effort if the solution required me to display a lot of self-confidence or even if it required me to put your interests ahead of mine. By choice, all I cared about was your thriving and I trusted that my own Life would be taken care of later, when results flourished.

"Only after I had that confident and humble frame of mind did I brainstorm about possible actions. Otherwise I wouldn't have been able to think outside the box enough to bring real Life for you. Lots of leaders shy away from the brave Life-giving decision, saying to themselves, 'Oh that solution's too hard.' But they fail to understand that investing in their people with confident humility is what makes Life explode. Most leaders don't need a bigger budget or a better title to make their teams' performance soar."

Looking down at the paper, Linda asked, "But how do you know that a potential action will work when you're brainstorming?"

"You can't know for sure that an action will produce Life until you execute the plan. When you're brainstorming, the best you can do is to come up with different options that are likely to bring Life, and then estimate which one will work best. Of course, you can always ask for other people's advice as you deliberate. For instance, I could have asked Adam if he thought you'd react positively to an opportunity to present in Boston. I also could have asked you directly before the trip if I had any doubts."

"Why didn't you ask me?"

"I didn't have doubts and I liked surprising you."

"Hmm." She smiled. "I'm assuming that the last of the three steps is self-explanatory. 'Execute the plan with confident humility' simply means that it's time to execute, right? Once you've figured out how Life can show up the most and you've invented a strategy to make it happen with confident humility, then you just have to do it."

Manny took his sweet time nodding his head. "Exx-aaact-ly. And when you've finished the steps, all that's left is to learn from your successes and mistakes for the next time around. When you're aiming for Life with confident humility, you'll succeed a lot, but sometimes you'll miss the mark. And that's okay because when folks get used to you humbly and intentionally trying to help them find Life at work, even when you fall short of your goal, people are super-forgiving. And ninety-nine percent of all mistakes are utterly correctable. Also, don't be afraid to ask your people if they're finding Life from the leadership decisions you've made. Ask them how you can improve for the next time around."

"So you basically repeat the three steps forever?"

"Yup. It's a lifestyle of repeating the three steps every time you make a decision. You ask yourself every morning, 'Where does Life want to show up today?' Soon you'll find your leadership influence growing as you understand more about the ways of Life. As long as you're being broken in, you'll never stop growing into a more effective leader. It takes commitment, but it's worth it. There's no other way in the long run to sustain your group at superior performance levels."

Manny pointed upward, as if he were about to make a significant claim. "But even beyond high performance and real results, your team will experience purpose, adventure and true community. There's no place in the world more exhilarating to be than on a team like that. No matter what industry you're in, your competitors can't duplicate that Life. It's your competitive advantage."

Thoughts fell into place and Linda shifted in her seat. She had learned to love being a part of the Blue Pod in the weeks prior. But now she understood that the group's new Life wouldn't have happened to such an extent had Manny not taken the time to break in his character.

"Linda, everywhere in the marketplace, people are longing for powerful leaders who are unafraid to be controlled by humility. A leader with strength under control is a mystery because the person exudes authority and humility all at once. This way of doing Life is a paradox. People don't know what to think at first, but they soon fall in love with the leader because they finally find the Life they've been longing for. When they sense, over time, that you're selflessly taking their interests into consideration along with your own, it unlocks their hearts and releases them to be selfless in pursuing the team's strategy. That's how you sustain a culture of breakthroughs.

"We can also see the beauty of this dynamic, of all places, in the Life of a wild horse. If you've ever been on a ranch, you know that it takes real collaboration for a horse and a rider to move together as one over difficult terrain. But how does that partnership get started? Well, a wild horse has to go through a training process when he's first brought into a stable. As they say on the ranch, the animal has to be broken in. The breaking-in process results in a steed that is receptive and responsive to the rider."

Manny fished through his bag and pulled out a paperback book. It was the children's tale *Black Beauty*. "I was reading to my kids one night when I came upon this passage where Anna Sewell describes the breaking-in process from the horse's perspective." Manny removed a bookmark and read aloud:

> **Everyone may not know what breaking in is, so I will describe it. It means to teach a horse to wear a saddle and bridle and to carry a rider on his or her back.**
>
> **The horse must also learn how to behave when pulling a cart. He must go fast or slow, just as the driver wishes. He must never rear up at something he sees, speak to other horses, or bite or kick.**

"You see, a wild stallion never loses any of his physical strength or prowess by being broken in. In fact his muscles and coordination only grow throughout the training. But the stallion learns to demonstrate his power under control. He becomes powerful in a selfless way for a greater purpose."

Manny confirmed that Linda was tracking, then said, "The wild horse represents a leader who's being broken in by a trainer called Life. Life is like the rider because you're learning how to carry or transport Life to new places at work. Your impulses come under your control as you increasingly take your cues from Life.

"Breaking in a stallion has to do with a saddle and a harness, but breaking in a leader has to do with learning to respect Life's ways until your choices, emotions and thoughts become aligned with Life. It takes training to form the habit of intentionally measuring your displays of power and restraint to encourage community, purpose and adventure." Manny furrowed his brow. "Is this making sense?"

As usual, Linda was on the ball. "The breaking-in process teaches you how to harness your wilder instincts and how to control your strength for the sake of conveying Life to others."

Manny wore a pleased look on his face. "A broken-in stallion can use his power to participate in the rider's higher agenda. An unruly horse can't tolerate a rider. An unruly leader can't participate in Life's higher agenda in the office. He's still valuable in an unruly kind of way, but he's not very useful to anybody but himself, thanks to his selfish impulses."

Manny's thoughts went to Jack for a moment. "Some leaders act like they sympathize with Life but they refuse to be broken in. Leaders like that lean heavily on their own understanding of the way things should be and pay little attention to Life's true requirements. They can't carry much Life to others. They balk at wearing the harness of humility. Their sensibilities are offended at the prospect of having a rider put any restraints on their impulses. They don't realize that all humans have a rider. If it's not Life, then it's Self-Concern.

"But a broken-in leader trains her mind and emotions to rise above Self-Concern. She has not only strength, but strength under the control of humility. She's able to command great authority precisely because she's disciplined in her power."

Linda had a new question. "How often do people mistake your confident humility for weakness?"

"It happens every now and then."

"What do you do in those situations?"

"On a good day, I won't respond by trying to prove my strength to them. On a bad day, I'll flex my muscles so that they'll know not to underestimate me. That never works. That's not too humble. The truth is that you really don't have to make a show of your strength because the people who underestimate you will eventually witness a moment when you rise up with great resolve. Then they'll see you display your strength for the right reasons. At that point they'll have to reconcile two thoughts in their minds. 'I thought this person was weak, but here I see they're really strong. What gives?' And that's when they start to discover the power of an executive with strength under control." He recalled a historical case in point. "I remember reading that Abraham Lincoln had people underestimate him all the time. Every now and then, people would mistake the president's humility as weakness, but they soon lived to regret their lack of judgment as they became acquainted with just how tenacious he was."

"Good example."

"I'm glad my high school history class was good for something." Manny checked his watch. "Let's wrap it up here." He looked at Linda, "I know I gave you a lot to consider. So would it be okay if I gave you a little homework assignment for next time?"

"No problem."

"Study Southwest Airlines. I doubt they'll use my terminology, but they've found a few interesting ways to operationalize confident humility across their entire organization. Employees are finding Life there in some amazing ways. Tell me what you find next time."

"Okay," Linda replied.

"And by the way, next time let's meet up with my friend Noah too. He's got some great insights on how to lead. I get together with him every week for lunch. Recently we've been bagging our lunches and 'dining' in Central Park. The ambience is quite nice if you don't mind shooing away the occasional bug."

"That would be great." They both got up and walked toward the double doors leading back inside.

Manny held the door open for Linda. "Making Life happen with confident humility isn't everything a leader needs to know, but it's the first and the last thing you should know. It's where you start. It's what you grow better at along the way, and it's the final criterion for evaluating whether you've been a good leader."

When Linda was back in her office, she typed the three steps of the breaking-in process into her notes, then added:

- **The core of being a good leader is intentionally having your strength under control in a way that generates Life (confident humility).**

- **When people trust you to take their interests into consideration along with your own, it unlocks their hearts and releases them to be selfless in pursuing the team's strategy. That's how you sustain a culture of breakthroughs.**

- **Breaking in a stallion has to do with a saddle and harness. Breaking in a leader has to do with developing your choices, emotions and thoughts so that you become aligned with Life. The end result is that you know how to intentionally measure your displays of power and restraint in every situation to encourage community, purpose and adventure in the people around you.**

- **All humans have a rider. Some of us serve the purposes of Life and some serve Self-Concern.**

- **Two dynamics happen simultaneously when a leader is being broken in: First, the selfish, impulsive side of the leader's will starts to disappear. At the same time, a mature character emerges and the leader's strengths are brought under control. As a result, the leader begins to rise above self-concern.**

- **People may sometimes misinterpret your confident humility as a sign of weakness.**

But it usually works to your advantage when people underestimate the reach of your inner intensity.

Later on, in Conference Room D, Linda endured three long rounds of interviews for the manager position. The first round was with Justin Floyd, the Green Pod's partner, and Jennifer Wynn, the outgoing manager. The second interview was with two associates from the pod. The third was with two partners from the Hiring and Promotions Committee.

Linda was pleased with both the answers she gave and the questions she asked. She had come up with some good questions the night before. Her mother had taught her that a wise person was recognized more by having insightful questions than by always having the right answer. Linda had no idea how the interviewers had perceived her, but she knew she'd given her best. Now all that was left was to allow the process to take its course. And pray.

❖   ❖   ❖

CHAPTER THIRTEEN

Wednesday found Linda in Greenville, South Carolina. It was just a day trip to do some interviews and collect some information about workflow at a client site. She took a morning flight there and planned on catching the four o'clock flight back in time for dinner in SoHo with friends. The company was a large manufacturer of automotive parts just off I-85, not far from the airport. The South was living up to its reputation: the people exuded politeness ("Sure good to have ya back, Ms. Flores"), and the day checked in at a humid ninety-one degrees.

Linda was escorted past the whirring and buzzing of the crowded factory floor and into a section of offices on the side. It was still noisy, but at least you could hear your own thoughts. She entered the corner office and sat down with Josh, the newly hired general manager in charge of the factory. He looked a little like Dick Clark and spoke with a slight Southern lilt. Like Dick Clark, he appeared to be about thirty years old, but his decades of experience said otherwise.

Josh recounted to Linda the challenges he'd faced in his first months on the job. About halfway through his story, it occurred to Linda that the way she saw business had changed. She was starting to see how the success or failure of a business depended on the presence or absence of confident humility in the people who ran the processes.

Josh was a prime example. He'd been hired for his expertise in making factories comply with some new and very stringent industry quality standards. Josh had to facilitate the factory's transition to a new assembly line system, but he first had to overcome some organizational impediments to change. Some of the employees liked doing things the old way just fine.

As he expected, sometimes he had to "flex his muscles" and use his authority to make his people embrace some of the more difficult aspects of the new system. One day, a few workers voiced their strong opinion that they should stop implementing a portion of the new system. Josh had to be firm with them. He admitted to Linda that he had to build up his confidence to do that. With humility and compassion, he expressed to the workers why they had to adhere to absolutely every aspect of the new system. "I know the new process is a little more complex than the current one, but I promise you the data you'll capture this way will decrease our error rate by seventeen to thirty-four percent. That's huge! So we've got to go ahead as planned."

On another day, Josh was walking around the floor, asking for input from people at all levels of the organization. The third-shift assembly line workers had a problem with the proposed location of a ventilator exhaust panel. Josh listened to the third-shift leader for forty-five minutes straight and still couldn't understand why the third shift was the only shift to object to the location. Nevertheless, Josh looked into an alternate location for the panel with the third shift leader and his management team. The modification to the plans would cost about $6,000 extra and have no impact on the floor's overall quality and efficiency metrics. Even though the proposed change didn't make rational sense as a capital investment, Josh decided to okay the modification as a human investment. The adjustment provided Josh with the buy-in of 139 employees on the third shift.

He found it irksome that he couldn't identify the "logical" reason to make the change, yet he still chose to proceed with the suggestion. He wasn't afraid to be self-effacing: he told the third shift, "I still don't see how this will make an impact on overall operations but I'll defer to you guys. After all, you're the ones out there on the floor all night long." The new system, along with the newly located exhaust panel, was finally implemented without a hitch. Everyone was satisfied and the facility's numbers improved dramatically.

Linda was impressed by how often confidence and humility were required to make Life happen in a factory. Linda had had a strong intellectual grasp of the concept, but now the notion began to make more intuitive sense. Life requires both power (tenacious confidence) and a system of checks and balances (humility) to ensure that a leader actually moves his teams and work results toward Life in a smart way. She asked, "Josh, have you ever stopped to consider how much confidence and humility play a role in your leadership?"

"Interesting question. I guess I've thought about it a little bit, but not in those words exactly," he replied. "The way I see it, everyone in a company needs everyone else because organizations have big problems and we each have a part of the solution. If I were to be timid or arrogant when I interact with people, then I wouldn't be effective at communicating my vision or aligning the groups with that vision. I'd fail to bring the different parts together for the whole solution."

"Your operations are now at the cutting edge of the industry." Cyrus & Hopkins had helped to make that possible, but Linda knew the lion's share of the credit was certainly due to Josh and his people. "Your facility is running at unprecedented levels of safety and efficiency. Your error rate is down. Profits are up because of the cost savings you've achieved. What was the hardest part of leading your people to make this breakthrough?"

"I'd probably have to say the hardest part for me was making sure my emotions didn't get in the way of our overall success.

When you're trying to change the way people do things, it's scary for them. They resisted my proposals. They resisted me. I had to realize that their resistance was just human nature. I had to convince my emotions that it had nothing to do with me or the quality of my presentation materials."

"How'd you do that?"

"I'd tell myself that there's no such thing as failure, there's only feedback. I'd walk into the conference room every week and start off by saying to the crowd, 'Look, we're all friends in this room. Let's talk about what you're afraid will happen and why these fears exist.' People would talk, they'd disagree with the new system and then I had to disagree with them. I'd say, 'This is why the system will work and this is how we can address your concerns.'"

Linda could tell how challenging all this must have been for Josh. "I'm sure it took a lot of confidence to get up there and talk despite all the objections that got flung at you. And I also know it takes a lot of humility to be friends with people after they try to tear your work to shreds."

"True, but it's worth it all. After you push and actually break through, you forget about all the effort it took. All you see is success. Friendships and results."

The meeting continued and Josh provided more details about what had been going on recently. Linda couldn't help but stand in awe at how one person's controlled strength had engineered a factory-wide breakthrough. In his first weeks on the job, Josh had exercised confident humility by regularly listening to others and trying to actually understand their points of view, even though he was rushed by project timelines. He tried to build consensus whenever possible but he was equally okay with making executive decisions if needed. Josh was even willing to be flexible midstream; he accommodated the third shift's adjustment to the exhaust panel halfway through the installation of the new system. Linda thought to herself, how could I not have noticed confident humility in action before? It's everywhere in an effective organization.

CHAPTER FOURTEEN

Meanwhile, up in Connecticut, Manny, Adam, Lee and Tom were spending the day with members of the Project X Task Force at Osanto's headquarters. The consultants had learned from their last trip and were wearing business casual attire. Manny, Lee and Tom were in the ground floor test kitchen, working with Frank DiLuna, the executive chef on the task force. They were cataloguing the number of menu items and rotating special items that would have to change with the introduction of trans-fat free oils. Adam was two floors above. He was reviewing marketing research data with Sarah Hunter, the director of marketing. The other associates were either traveling like Linda or back at the firm working on other client assignments. The pod was stretched thin between all the work.

At one point during the day, Manny wanted to go outside for a fresh-air break. He was intending to stay for only a minute or two, so he didn't go far. He stepped out under a cloudless sky and stood a few feet away from the entrance to the lobby. The days were mercifully growing warmer and warmer. He took in the sun and the distant melodies coming from the ridge of trees at the end of the parking lot. The birds were doing their thing. The trees threw speckled shadows over the grass and underbrush.

Manny's thoughts turned to Jack in Florida. Typically, whenever he considered Jack those days, a wave of disappointment accompanied his thoughts. That day was no different. Why was Jack being so difficult to work with? But in the midst of his contemplation, Manny decided to climb out of the pool of disenchantment he'd been swimming in. He'd done enough swimming that week. He was not a fan of dwelling in negativity for too long.

He set his mind on finding the positive. It took him a couple of seconds, but it finally came. Jack wasn't all bad news. He'd been working really hard to bring home the bacon. Jack had done a better job of finding new clients than had most of the firm's partners. Even back at Columbia, Jack had always excelled at enrolling Manny and the other students into whatever the harebrained prank of the day was.

As Manny searched his feelings, he realized he was envious of Jack getting to relax at a resort. But he then remembered that those conferences usually aren't that enjoyable when most of the time you're consumed in the alchemy of trying to convert strangers into clients. Jack happened to be in a resort, but he was working hard. He was providing something that Manny and the pod needed a lot. I should be thankful, Manny thought. I am thankful. I need to be careful not to write Jack off as irrelevant to the pod and my job.

Manny then noticed a woman, presumably an Osanto's employee, shut her car door and approach the building. She was completely bald. Manny scrambled to open the door for her and forgot to breathe. The absence of eyebrow hair and eyelashes confirmed Manny's suspicion. Suddenly, Manny was eight years old again.

Caleb was handsome, athletic, smart and kind. Quite a giddy combination for any normal thirteen-year old to handle, but then again, Caleb was beyond normal. Every girl in Overland Park, Kansas wanted to date him. Every boy wanted to hang out with him, especially his eight-year-old brother. Little Manny adored him. Fortunately for Manny, Caleb let him tag along almost everywhere. You could often find the Johnson boys walking down the road in the afternoon, Caleb's arm draped across Manny's little shoulders. They fought from time to time like all boys do, but within a minute they'd be back together again, playing catch with a baseball or whatever other game they felt like.

Caleb made time to throw around a baseball or frisbee with Manny every single day. This was no small thing to do when you're juggling soccer practice, youth group meetings, clarinet lessons, homework and, of course, school. The two shared a tight bond. That was why Caleb's world was turned upside down when the symptoms began. Plain tiredness was the first. It was a big deal when Manny felt too weak to play ball for four days in a row. Nosebleeds became frequent. Then Manny arrived home from school with leg pains almost every day. "You okay, pal?" was the first thing Caleb would ask when Manny came in the door. Manny never had it in him to lie to Caleb, so he responded frankly.

The next weeks were filled with fevers, night sweats, headaches, infections and plenty of visits to the hospital. Long names like acute lymphoblastic leukemia should never be uttered in the same breath as your little brother's name, yet that's exactly what the doctors did. To be more accurate, they mostly said 'ALL,' the abbreviation for the cancer that was in Manny's bone marrow. Manny endured what seemed to be a never-ending cycle of going to the hospital every month for chemotherapy and then spending ages in bed recovering. His skin became ashy and wan. The sparkle in his golden eyes grew dim from chronic fatigue.

Mom and Dad became the world's most faithful caretakers. They cleaned Manny, entertained him at his bedside, prayed with him and made sure he took his medicines on time. Manny lost a noticeable amount of weight and sometimes had signs of dehydration. As for Caleb, he made sure Manny's water bottle was always full. He also took it upon himself to become Manny's nutritionist. Dad and Mom recognized that Caleb desperately wanted to participate with them in taking care of Manny, so they trained him to help Mom prepare the food. The doctor had instructed them to cook meats well and to avoid fresh vegetables and fruits. Chemotherapy had weakened Manny's immune system, so he easily got sick from bacteria— apparently it's hard to wash absolutely all the bacteria off of fresh fruits and vegetables.

After school each day, Caleb got to bring the dinner tray up to Manny's room. Manny was seldom hungry after chemo, so it secretly delighted Caleb that sometimes he was the only one who could convince his little brother to open his mouth. Caleb would sit on the edge of the bed and patiently serve each spoonful. He wouldn't leave until the bowl was empty, even when his friends were calling and Dad was right there to take over the feeding.

When you're eight, you have no idea how to interpret the fact that your hair is falling out in large clumps. For Manny it meant that everyone instantly knew that something was wrong with him on the days he felt good enough to go outside. Mom shaved his head all the way down to soften his appearance. The look on Manny's face was unforgettable the day that Mom, Dad and Caleb came into Manny's room with smiles on their faces and not a single hair on their heads. Even Mom! They had all shaved their heads bald as a sign of love and solidarity. Mom could hardly wait to exclaim, "It was Caleb's idea!"

One time, Mom and Dad were awakened in the middle of the night to the sounds of Manny weeping. Often the anti-nausea medicine didn't work so well. Manny was doubled over in his bed, his pajamas and sheets swimming in a layer of foul-smelling vomit. Dad darted to the bathroom to grab some towels. Mom was in the middle of wiping the orange paste from Manny's neck with kleenex when Caleb streaked through the air. He flew past her and landed to the left of Manny.

When Dad came back, armed with the towels, Mom turned toward her husband. No words needed to be spoken. They both observed through watery eyes Caleb's body wrapped around Manny's soaked frame. Caleb paid no attention to the vomit or the smell. Nothing else mattered. He held Manny until Manny stopped crying. Mom and Dad held each other and felt their hearts swell. This was one of several seasons when grief and joy comingled unexpectedly in the Johnson family. Manny fell asleep in his brother's arms. They had to wake Manny long enough to clean him in the bathtub. He eventually fell asleep again in between Mom and Dad in their bed. Caleb fell asleep in between them too. It was crowded but nobody seemed to mind.

Like most boys of thirteen, Caleb was never one to dwell on the past. He lived thoroughly in the present, savoring each day as it came. But soon he found his imagination pulled toward a dark potential future, a future with no Manny to brighten it. It became hard for Caleb to dwell in any place but the past—the only place that contained the good times he longed for.

Seven months after Manny's first symptoms, the Johnson family's miracle arrived. The doctors confirmed that Manny was completely healed. Caleb's relief was nothing short of monumental, as could be expected. Manny would go on to have a long and full Life after all. How ironic, the way things worked out, that Caleb was actually the one whose Life would be cut far too short by a car accident.

"Thank you so much," the bald woman said as she stepped into the lobby. Manny was still holding the door open a full minute after she had gone inside. He remembered to breathe again. He had gone through the fire in his childhood and survived. His passionate pursuit of Life had been imprinted on him when he was closest to death. He'd learned how to give Life to others from a council of experts—Caleb, Mom and Dad. It's a no brainer, Manny thought as he entered the lobby, the best stuff I have to offer all came from home.

Upstairs, Adam was arched over a dozen open files on a desk in the marketing department. He turned next door to Sarah Hunter to see if she wanted anything from the vending machine.

She was poring over her own stack of files. "No thanks, I'm good. Just walk down the hall, make a right and you'll see the machine by the water fountain."

"Thanks," he said as he stood up and headed toward the machine. The brief walk would afford him the time alone he wanted. He needed to deliberate over what to do with his significant discovery. His Blackberry rang as he tried to slide his crumpled dollar bill into the machine's receiver for the second time. Hmm. Jack Jameson.

The next day, Thursday, started off with the usual status meeting. Every morning so far, the task force and whatever pod members were on site gathered in a conference room to go over the progress they had made. Manny usually brought some fruit and muffins for people to nibble on. So far, the forty-five minute meetings had been fairly routine. There was nothing really interesting to share yet. The project was fresh, and brilliant findings took time. Today was somewhat special though, since Ricky would be joining the group at the end of the meeting. He was expecting a status report. The group had agreed that two people would jointly give the overview to Ricky. Sarah Hunter would speak for Osanto's and Lee would speak for Cyrus & Hopkins.

The status meeting proceeded normally. Linda had joined the group again, back from Greenville. Manny had his legs crossed and was fiddling with a pen. They covered the usual things, and then Ricky finally came. He shook hands and laughed it up with everyone. The room then got quiet except for the appointed speakers. Lee and Sarah did a good job. Manny wrote down some feedback to discuss later with Lee. At the end, the two concluded their remarks and Ricky got up from his chair to depart.

"Sir," said Adam.

"Yes."

"Just one more thing before you go."

"Oh." Ricky said with a smile, sitting down again.

Adam sighed. "There may be a trend. It may be nothing at all but I found it yesterday and, really, it may be nothing but I was thinking perhaps I should share it." Under the table, Manny was patting his hand against the side of his pants.

Ricky invited him to speak, looking to Manny to see whether this was a planned part of the morning. Manny just raised his eyebrows, shrugged his shoulders and smiled. That crazy Adam is full of surprises.

Adam went on, "Well sir, as we all know, Osanto's main target market is the business lunch and dinner crowd. So it makes sense that the majority of your branches are located in central business districts across the three states. I had a hunch, so I looked at the market research that Sarah gave me. I think I found a trend of higher demand for the healthier items in the few restaurants that are not in a central business district."

"That's common knowledge," Sarah interjected.

"True. However, I took the liberty of calling up the managers in those branches and it turns out that the typical healthy order is a take-out order."

"That's still common knowledge."

"Yes, but then I looked at the demand numbers again and cross-referenced a map. I think all the branches that are succeeding with the healthy items are near to what I call hot spots—an airport, a major hospital or a shopping mall. The healthy items aren't selling as well in restaurants far away from a hotspot."

"So what do you make of this?" asked Ricky.

"Well, since Osanto's is already moving toward a healthier menu, why not capitalize on the health-minded customers in the hotspots."

"Go on." Ricky leaned forward and clasped his fingers on the table in front of him. "I'm listening."

"My guess is that people can't easily find food that's both tasty and healthy in most airports, so they're picking it up from your restaurants and bringing it with them. And even though you should be able to find healthy food in a hospital cafeteria, you can't find healthy comfort food that tastes great. So the patients' families are bringing Osanto's food into the hospitals. And it's a similar story for customers in the shopping malls. They can't find healthy food that tastes good there, so they go to the nearest Osanto's. Your branches that are close to malls have a larger than usual demand for healthy meal sit-down service."

Adam paused to make sure Ricky was following him. "These hotspots have a built-in demand for healthy food that's delicious. If further research proves my hunch is right, I have three options for you. First, Osanto's should increase its take-out menu promotions around hot spots. Second, you could open more branches near hot spots. Third, and most important, maybe it's time to consider establishing Osanto's Express. It would be a smaller, limited menu, food-court version of your restaurant and we'd locate them in airports, hospitals and shopping malls. This would expand your customer base, make use of your new healthier menu and increase profits."

Ricky was visibly impressed. Sarah and several other task force members were visibly peeved. Manny was making crisis management plans.

"Hold off on everything else," Ricky instructed the task force, rising from his chair. "Follow up on Adam's idea and put together an Osanto's Express proposal." He walked toward the door, stopped and turned back toward the group. "As soon as possible." The meeting broke up and everyone scrambled out of their chairs.

Manny chased down Sarah and caught up with her by her office. He went inside, closed the door and emerged into the hallway thirty minutes later. He'd done all the damage control he could, but he wasn't certain his efforts would make enough of a difference to save the pod's relationship with the task force. Adam had blindsided everyone and Manny never saw it coming. Manny's first solo project at the firm was, in some ways, disintegrating.

Adam had partaken in the hallowed Cyrus & Hopkins pastime known as grandstanding. You hold on to information. Keep your colleagues in the dark. You hold your cards close to the vest until the time is right to dazzle the big shots with your stunning brilliance. It was a common practice among consultants at the firm, but it hadn't been the practice of the Blue Pod since Manny had arrived.

Manny strode down the corridor intently, his face red with anger, until he reached the men's room. He pushed the door out of his way, scanned under the toilet doors and approached the sink area. He was alone. He grasped both sides of a sink, shut his eyes and released a hair-raising cry.

After a moment, he opened his eyes again and stared at his reflection in the mirror. He replayed Adam's words in his mind and cringed. He thought of the ways that he could have responded to Adam during the meeting—ways to put Adam in his place and allow the task force to save face. But, of course, he hadn't said anything during the meeting.

Manny glimpsed the trash receptacle out of the corner of his eye. He wanted to kick it with all his might. He tensed his thigh in preparation, but ultimately resisted the urge. Mangled garbage cans don't usually help a consultant's reputation much.

Instead, by sheer force of habit, he decided to do what he felt least like doing: he took a deep breath and contemplated how Life could show up, given the turn of events. How could Life now be revealed in the task force, the overall project, and yes, even in Adam? He concluded that confronting Adam was the best option to start with. Manny heard the creak of the men's room door, followed by footsteps. It didn't matter to him. He didn't need more time alone. He released the sink. Time to execute.

Adam was in the test kitchen interviewing three chefs. It was a large industrial kitchen decked out in stainless steel and white tile. Manny walked in and invited Adam for a walk out back by the duck pond. Adam excused himself from the chefs.

As the two were walking, Manny made an assessment of the situation one more time. He was proud of the fact that he hadn't torn Adam's head off yet. They were walking on the grass by the pond when Manny simply asked, "Why did you do what you did back there?"

Adam considered responding by asking Manny if he was talking about the chef interviews, but he thought better of it. "I just got the idea yesterday. I wasn't sure if it would fly or not."

"You hid crucial information from me. You disregarded my instructions to share everything with the task force. You could have said something during the status meeting before Ricky came. Instead you took all the glory for yourself. I had to apologize to Sarah for nearly half an hour before she could believe that I didn't put you up to the stunt you pulled."

"It was just business. Nothing personal," Adam said. "What I said moved the project forward."

"You're fired, you ass!" That was what Manny honestly felt like saying. But actually, he didn't. Instead, he summoned a measure of self-control and bit his tongue. What he really said was, "Adam, your idea was good, but that's not why we're out here surrounded by ducks, now is it? I told you not to keep vital information to yourself since we didn't want the task force to view us as competition. Do you have any idea how far you've set us back? They see us as a major threat now and they may not want to share their information with us anymore. How's that going to help our work here for the rest of the project? I wanted them to know that we're the kind of consultants who let our friends get the glory before we do. Instead, now they're worrying that their boss thinks they're idiots because an outsider had to teach them how to run their own business."

Adam's temperature was rising. "They'll get over it. Can't you see that Ricky's happy? Why can't you be happy too?" He was shouting now. "Why are the little things always such a big deal to you?" The ducks started to migrate gracefully toward the far side of the pond.

Manny bellowed, "Because the little things are the big things!" The ducks now flew off toward the woods. "Don't act like you never knew that you were supposed to be collaborating with the task force—that was your *job* for this assignment, after all. Or is fulfilling your job responsibilities a little thing to you? You blindsided the task force members. That's not little either. And don't forget that Ricky is asking those guys for their opinion as to whether we get the national contract."

"Well, Ricky may not need much of their input now that he knows that we can deliver results. Maybe now we have half a chance to get the contract because the credit won't be dissipated across some task force who never came up with the idea themselves in the first place. Everyone else at our firm is fine with this type of thing. It's just business!"

"It's never just business when you're dealing with people's lives." Manny stepped closer, put a hand on Adam's shoulder and looked him straight in the eyes. "Adam, I know this is hard to hear right now, but this would be a great time for you to embrace the humility we talked about on Monday."

Adam turned away and walked off a few steps closer to the pond. Manny let him go. After a few seconds Manny asked, "What did you mean when you said everyone at the firm is fine with this?"

Adam sheepishly turned around and shrugged, not daring to meet Manny's eyes. "Jack thinks it's okay."

"What?"

"Jack called me from Florida yesterday to ask how things were going. I mentioned the anomaly I found in the data. He told me that I should keep it under wraps until I was in front of Ricky. He said it was the best way for us to get the national contract."

Now Manny had his turn at walking away a few paces. He ran his hand through his hair and sighed, looking up to the sky. The fact that Jack was undermining his authority and poisoning the situation disturbed him more than he wanted to admit. Why hadn't Jack called Manny for an update? For a moment, Manny had no idea what to say to Adam. Then the moment passed. Manny turned around. "I'm the one on the front lines, not Jack. I'm the one who expressly told the pod not to withhold any information. I'm the one who gave Sarah my personal word that we'd become a seamless part of her task force and that they'd know everything we knew. Jack got it wrong. He doesn't fully know the dynamics going on here, so he called it wrong. Adam, you should have known better. You have to apologize to Sarah and the team."

"What?!"

"Apologize and do whatever it takes to earn back the trust of the task force. Don't do it just because it makes good business sense. Do it because it's right."

"You have *got* to be kidding me!" But Manny's eyes told a different story. "Look Manny, I value your integrity, but—"

"Don't value it! Just do it, Adam. Do what's right."

Adam just stared back. It wasn't a look of defiance, but it wasn't a look of acceptance either.

Manny took a moment to figure out a way to be heard. "Look, you like the way I lead. You like when I invest in developing you as a professional. You like the fun new culture of the pod.

You like it when I'm humble before you, but you think it's immaterial whether you do the same. Well, leadership is not a spectator sport. We all have to lead from wherever we are in the organization otherwise it doesn't work. Now it's your turn. Do what's right." Manny turned and headed toward the building, taking large strides. Adam remained motionless for a few seconds but then ran to catch up when Manny was halfway back to the door.

As they approached the entrance, Manny turned to look at him. "Adam, I've told you what humility requires. This is the point where you decide who you want to be when you grow up. Either you can be like Jack or you can be like me."

CHAPTER FIFTEEN

It was Friday morning, and almost all the pod was back at the office. That's the way it always seemed to work out. No matter how much travel the consultants did during a week, they always scheduled themselves to be back in New York on Fridays if at all possible. Most consultants wanted at least the semblance of a normal life. When you're a road warrior, three whole nights of sleeping in your own bed toward the week's end can be priceless. Jack, however, was still in Florida, schmoozing potential clients at the big multi-industry conference.

Linda walked up one flight of stairs to the twenty-sixth floor. She was feeling a little nervous. She walked around the corner of the hallway and stopped in front of the little plaque that read "Bernadette Waters." Linda popped her head in the doorway of the competition's office. "How's it going?" Bernadette smiled from behind her freckles and invited Linda to take a seat. The ladies dove into all the details that chitchat invited: the weather, how the current project's doing, the rumor of a new mega-client that the Red Pod was about to engage. Both consultants were friendly, yet there was a slight current of tension running behind all the pleasantness. They were acquaintances who had spoken with each other in passing at firm cocktail parties, yet they'd never had a real face-to-face before. And now here was Linda, sitting in

Bernadette's office, sizing her up. And here was Bernadette, sizing Linda up. They both knew the other had applied for the Green Pod position. Neither of them talked about the fact. Yet the truth was there in the air between them, coloring all that was said and unsaid. Linda felt as if she'd done a charitable act for both of them by stopping by. Each wanted to know a little more about the person she was up against. Bernadette also wanted to hear stories from someone who worked directly for Manny, the talk of the firm. Linda shared the story of how the box of koosh balls ended up a permanent fixture in Conference Room B.

Linda left the office with nothing but good impressions in her mind. Bernadette was friendly enough. She was eloquent and detail-oriented. Her extensive connections in the technology world could serve the Green Pod well since they were known for getting the bulk of the IT-related assignments in the firm. Linda was no slouch in the technology area herself, but she knew that Bernadette would probably look better on paper.

In a way, Linda was disappointed that her red-haired counterpart was so gracious and accomplished. Bernadette and her husband lived with and took care of her elderly father, who struggled with dementia. She also had surprisingly good ideas about where the firm should be headed in the economy's changing landscape. It would have been so much easier to despise Bernadette had she been an ornery, incompetent buffoon. But she wasn't. This race was too close to call. Linda walked back down the stairs. She exhaled and tucked a wisp of hair behind her ear. She truly wanted this promotion.

Manny noticed Linda as he was leaving the library. He was walking in the opposite direction and said, "I put a copy of my recommendation letter on your desk."

"Thanks, Manny." She was grateful indeed, but it did little to calm her nerves now that she had encountered her formidable opponent.

Manny was almost back to his office when he heard Deborah Hopkins's voice. "Can you spare a minute?" They both ended up walking back to her office. It was Manny's first time inside it. Her walls were flanked with several paintings from the firm collection and dozens of smaller pictures of Deborah shaking hands with presidents, CEOs and celebrities. There were two potted trees bordering her desk.

Deborah asked how Manny was adjusting to life at Cyrus & Hopkins. He told her that he was enjoying his time there, especially since the Blue Pod dynamics were improving.

Eventually she made her way to asking how things were going with "that restaurant." Manny gave her an update, mentioning Adam's great market insight and Ricky's keen interest in Adam's recommendations. Deborah was satisfied. "Good. Keep me abreast of how things go, especially if you hear anything about the national account."

The rest of the day passed without much to mention. The pod meeting was uneventful. Adam was quiet the whole time. Manny got caught up on paperwork afterwards. Rachel looked over the pod's time reports for that week and emailed them to Jack.

At eleven that night, Adam was sitting in his office, rolling his head around on his shoulders. Something popped in his neck the way he intended it to and he resumed his position over his laptop. He was working on an overview of what he'd uncovered so far about Osanto's market demographics and his hotspot theory. He was finding it hard to find the right words. He realized while rubbing his eyes that perhaps the words were elusive because he was drained.

When he opened his eyes again he was startled to see the blurred outline of a man standing in his doorway. "Manny," he said as his eyes came back into focus. "I didn't see you."

"Hi." Manny leaned against the doorframe.

They lingered in awkward silence, neither knowing what to say. Manny had had his fill of drama for the day. He was evaluating whether a conflict-free discussion could be in the cards. Finally he dove in. "You're not working on Osanto stuff now, are you?"

"Yeah. I, uh, need to put my thoughts down for Sarah Hunter."

"Oh."

Another silence.

Adam spoke but he couldn't lift his eyes. "You ask for very hard things."

"I know."

"Before I left Osanto's today, I went to Sarah Hunter and apologized. I told her that I temporarily got wrapped up in myself. I assured her that you didn't know anything about my grandstanding. I think she accepted my apology."

"She did." Sarah had called Manny earlier and told him. Apparently Adam had gone to the offices of each of the task force members and apologized. He'd also done the same with the pod members on site. Manny wished Adam would look up to see the respect and compassion he had in his eyes. "Are you okay?"

"Yeah," Adam said smiling and finally looking up, a little surprised that his boss would care.

"Good." Manny was wondering how Life could possibly show up next. He got it. Manny closed the door far enough to reach around and yank Adam's blazer from its hangar on the coat hook. "You've suffered enough today. Let's grab a beer."

Adam raised his hands in protest. "I've got lots of work here." He raised his eyebrows. "One of my bosses had this great idea of cramming an extra client into our pod's agenda."

"Alright, alright," Manny laughed. "I guess if I have the power to make work materialize then I also have the power to make it disappear." He walked over to the desk and held up the coat as a visual plea. Adam sighed in resignation and saved his work. He stood up, stuck an arm through the sleeve and stepped into the blazer that Manny was holding.

They wandered a few blocks south into gleaming Times Square, where even at night it was daytime. They found the place with the exterior walls of glass on the corner of 47th and Broadway. Inside, the buzz was palpable. It was hard to find a spot to sit, but Adam snagged a barstool next to an elevated counter against the glass wall facing Broadway. Manny held a frosty glass mug of beer in each hand and zigzagged through yuppies, bikers and three Swedish tourists in animated conversation. Adam managed to grab another stool just as Manny appeared. They rested themselves on the barstools and placed their mugs on the counter. They spent a moment just peering through the glass wall, watching the recently paroled theatre crowds whizzing by mere feet away.

Adam had a grave look about him. He finally said it. "I fell for one of those lies, didn't I?"

"What lies?" Manny inquired, looking over the rim of his mug.

"You said that arrogance happens when someone lives out a lie. So which of the two lies was it?"

Manny took a long sip before responding. "You made the mistake of believing that you were more important than the others on the task force. But when you chose confident humility and made amends, you rejected the lie and limited its damage. I'm proud of you." Adam didn't look up. He was slouched over the counter, staring at the multitudes. "Adam, you're a brilliant consultant. But that's not what impresses me most. All the brilliance in the world means nothing unless you've got the guts to do good with it. By being selfless, you showed yourself to be the man I hoped you were." Manny took another long draw. "*That's* why I'm proud of you."

Adam shook his head. "Don't be proud of me. It was so hard to admit to the clients and co-workers that I don't do things the way I should. It was really hard. You want a high level of credibility, you know?"

"Adam." Manny waited until he looked back. "Don't you see that your credibility has increased since you apologized? Nobody does something that gut-wrenchingly valiant by accident. Now we can trust you to do what's right, even if you mess up at first. We never knew that before. That kind of credibility is much more valuable than looking perfect all the time. News flash: everybody knows that nobody's perfect. So when you run into someone with the audacity to own up to his mistakes, well, that's everything. It's like I told Sarah when she called earlier tonight: now we can trust you for the ego-surrender it takes to collaborate."

"So even with all that happened today, you still think you see humility in me?" There was more than a hint of disbelief in his voice.

"Heck yeah. You're doing pretty good. I've seen far worse cases. You know the opposite of confidence and humility are fear and selfish pride. Fear and pride have caused a lot of executives to live out a lie to the point where they refuse to be taught by Life. They reject the confident humility they need to change. When they get to that point, no one else can teach them how to grow into a better leader, a better friend or a better spouse."

"So that's it? They're hopeless?

"Well, I wouldn't say they were hopeless, but I will say that their only hope isn't a pleasant option. Only suffering can teach them."

"Suffering?"

"Yes. Suffering. Only two things can bypass a person's intellectual defenses and directly penetrate their heart: beauty and suffering. Seeing beauty can inspire confident humility and Life within you if you have a teachable heart. But when you're happily lost in a lie and you reject confident humility, that leaves suffering as the only way that Life can shock you into positive growth. I once had a friend who was, shall we say, humility-challenged. He had a major heart attack and barely survived. His wife and children almost lost him. The ordeal caused him to humbly re-evaluate his priorities during the months of recovery following his bypass surgery. The same kind of humbling happened to another friend of mine when she was abruptly fired from her position as the director of a large nonprofit. She spent months trying to identify the patterns of fear and pride that had derailed her career. That kind of suffering can penetrate the heart and cause you to re-think things. Suddenly, a hard-hearted executive has a new openness and sensitivity to learn Life's lessons. That's why I say that you're humble, Adam. You didn't need a huge dose of affliction in order to grow. You were teachable. You just needed a strong conversation."

"I've never thought of slicing and dicing my decision-making that way."

Manny raised his mug. "Here's to all those who choose to lose their pride and starve their fears."

Adam straightened up and raised his mug for the toast. "Thanks, Coach."

Stars shone overhead. It didn't matter that they were sparkling from the video billboard outside.

PART FIVE

❖ ❖ ❖

The Gamble

CHAPTER SIXTEEN

Linda was ensconced among the many pillows in her picture-window nook. The living room of her pre-war apartment overlooked the harbor, lower Manhattan, the South Street Seaport and the Brooklyn Bridge as well. She was dressed in a bathrobe, taking a bite of her bagel every now and then. She hugged her knees, rotating her eyes every few seconds between the morning sky and the morning news on television. This was her weekday morning routine. She started to thumb through a copy of the *Economist* when she realized that she was trying to distract herself from thinking about the day ahead. The Hiring and Promotions Committee would likely be announcing that day whether or not she would be the next manager of the Green Pod. She was a little nervous.

Wrapped in thought, a voice from the ignored television caught her attention. The newscaster had said something about "an ultimate act of humility and sportsmanship." Linda looked at the screen.

The announcer was speaking about Sarah Tulchosky, a college softball player for Western Oregon University. The screen flashed a montage of pictures of Sarah playing on the softball field. Apparently she was in her last year of college, and after four long years of playing, she had finally managed to hit her first home run. Just as she was approaching first base, Sarah collapsed on the ground. Something bad had happened. It was later confirmed that a ligament in her knee had torn.

Sarah's teammates proposed to carry her around the bases so she could complete her momentous home run. However, the umpires refused to allow it, citing the rules of the game. And that was the point when something incredible happened. Someone from the *opposing* team volunteered to carry her instead. Apparently nothing in the rules prevented the opposing team from carrying Sarah.

The person who came up with the idea was Mallory Holtman, a first baseman and a career leader in home runs for Central Washington University. Mallory got together with shortstop Liz Wallace and linked arms. Sarah sat down. They supported Sarah's weight between themselves and slowly went around the bases. They made stops to let Sarah's left foot touch each base. All three got the giggles every time they did.

Sarah's home run ended up winning the game for her team. Needless to say, the fans gave a standing ovation when the young women arrived at home plate and delivered Sarah safely into her teammates' open arms. It may have been the slowest and most crowded home run in the history of softball. Afterwards, Mallory and Liz went back to their positions and did their best to win during the remainder of the game.

"Wow," was all Linda could voice as she turned off the TV and walked to the bedroom to get ready for the day. Gears were turning in her mind. She noted that Mallory probably felt confident as a player since she was a career leader in home runs for her school. She didn't have anything to prove to herself. As a result, she didn't consider herself above the task of humbly sacrificing her personal interests to bring Life to Sarah. And now, that simple expression of confident humility had produced so much Life that Linda felt its impact thousands of miles away in New York City.

Linda showered, dressed and was ready to go, but for some reason she found herself sitting on the couch instead of going out the door. Vague feelings were stirring deep inside. Of course, it had to do with her potential promotion. But what exactly? There was nervousness there, yes. Anticipation too. But there was more. She checked in with herself and isolated the intuition. Something wasn't quite right. A cautionary nugget of wisdom. Some action was required. She continued her introspection and reached a conclusion. She heard herself speaking aloud. "The first step is to discover how Life wants to show up…"

Across town, Rachel had just left her apartment for her morning jog. She had always been conscious of the benefits of exercise. She was whisking past rows of flowers on display in front of a deli on the Upper East Side. Her mobile phone vibrated. "Hi Jack. You in the office already?" She was trying not to pant too hard into the receiver.

"No," he replied. "Actually, I've extended my time here in Florida. The main part of the conference is over but there are still lots of potential clients around. A few more post-conference break-out sessions are going on today and tomorrow."

"When will you be back?"

"Either tomorrow or Wednesday."

"Did you get the brochure I emailed you?" A mock-up of the new firm brochure had been released to all the partners for their review. Since Jack was out of town, Rachel had sent an electronic version of it to him. The brochure had five pictures of consultants at work. Most of them were staged action shots. Jack was in one of them pretending to explain something to a team of executives. These "executives" were actually New York actors who were happy to get any paying gig besides being extras on *Law & Order* again.

"Yes, I got it, but I don't know why they chose *that* shot of me for the brochure. Anyhow, I suppose I look okay."

"You look fine," Rachel comforted him. "I'm sure they can photoshop out the angst from your face."

Jack decided to move on to a more pressing matter. "Rachel, I think there was an error in the time reports you sent."

"Oh? I always cut and paste the numbers straight from the computer. There shouldn't be any errors."

"But the reports say that the entire pod spent almost all their time on the Osanto's project last week."

"That's right."

There was a long, pregnant silence.

Whenever Jack went quiet, it usually meant something really good or really bad. This didn't quite seem like one of the good times to Rachel. The truth was that Jack was swearing silently. He had grossly underestimated Manny and the pod. While he was in Florida, Jack had incorrectly assumed that, at most, two or three of his overworked associates would be insane enough to volunteer for extra work. Two or three at most. He hadn't even thought to confirm the numbers when he had called Adam in Connecticut.

Jack's mind was reeling. Manny had succeeded in hijacking all of Jack's troops for a trivial mission. Base camp had been deserted for a whole week. How could a Johnny-come-lately manager outmaneuver Jack, a Cyrus & Hopkins partner? Had Manny stolen the pod's loyalty away from him?

"Jack, are you still there?"

"Yes."

"I thought maybe the phone service cut out or something." Rachel laughed nervously.

"I have to go." Then he disconnected.

Rachel stared at her phone and stuck it back in her pocket. Before resuming her jog, she spoke to the unsuspecting Korean man arranging the flowers in front of the deli. "And they wonder why I need vodka at my desk!"

CHAPTER SEVENTEEN

Meanwhile, over in Queens, Manny reached up and steadied himself with the metal handle overhead. The jostling subway car was crowded. He was making his way toward Manhattan on the elevated tracks of the 7 line. The colorful establishments of Sunnyside whizzed by below. Amidst the hubbub of the train, he didn't hear the familiar chime indicating he'd received a text message on his phone—a message from Jack. The subway proceeded into the tunnel under the East River.

Elevator doors opened at Cyrus & Hopkins about twenty minutes later. Manny appeared and greeted Louise the reception-ist. "How's it going today?" Louise was all too happy to have someone ask her since most people in the office tended to ignore her. She was one of those people who was always trying to make you come to one of her events.

She was beaming. "My morning has been faaaah-bulous. I've been putting the final touches on a fund-raising party for the anti-road rage club that my sister's boyfriend's colleague introduced me to last winter when…" Manny's mobile phone rang in the middle of her discourse. "Anyway, you should definitely come."

He excused himself, picked up his phone and headed for his office, secretly grateful for the interruption. "Hi."

"Manny. Sorry to call you this early. I was going to leave a voicemail message."

"Morning, Ricky. No problem. I'm in the office already. How are you?"

"Couldn't be better. Last night, Sarah Hunter gave me the task force's recommendations for Osanto's Express. I'm in love with the plan." Manny walked into his office and saw a copy of the report on his desk. Adam and Lee had worked on it over the weekend with Sarah and a few others in Connecticut. The report had elaborated on the initial ideas that Adam had presented. Manny had kept tabs on the report's progress by phone over the weekend.

"Glad you like it, Ricky. I think you've got a real opportunity here."

"I'm going to start up the corporate machinery to get approval for capital expenditures. Can you guys come back this afternoon to help us flesh out the business plan? Say, around two or three?"

"We'll be there," Manny said with a smile. They discussed the report further and covered some housekeeping details as Manny walked down to Linda's office. Linda waved at Manny when he walked in. He sat down in one of her chairs, brought his phone conversation to a close and hung up. Turning to Linda, he said, "Ricky's so excited, he's about to explode! He likes the proposal. My gut tells me that he's almost ready to recommend us for the big-boy project next week when he goes to the parent company's national initiative meetings."

"That's great!" Linda said, glancing at her watch. "Should we get going though?" They were scheduled to meet up with Noah at eight so they could be back in the office before nine.

"Let's do it." Manny slid his phone back into his pocket without looking at it. They went downstairs, journeyed past the statue of Columbus and through the regal gates of Central Park.

Once inside, they crossed the interior roadway, continued along a narrow path and approached a huge gray rock jutting out of the earth. Noah was sitting on top of it. His arms were behind him, propping up his body. He was obviously enjoying the warmth of the sunlight as it fell on his face.

There were several clusters of rocks like this one scattered through the park. They were often crowded at lunchtime. Time spent on a rock, surrounded by trees, was like a vacation from work in the middle of the day.

This particular rock was about forty feet long and about fifteen feet tall at its highest point. It was somewhat flat on the top and its contours made for an easy climb. This was good news for Linda who had to scale it in heels.

"It's great to meet you after hearing so much about you," Noah said, getting up and offering a hand to help her up.

She took his hand. "Has Manny been talking about me?"

"Yes he has. He's been filling me in on your rise as a leader."

She looked to Manny, who was taking a seat on a large blanket that Noah had spread. "My rise?" Manny shrugged his shoulders with a whimsical look.

Linda and Noah joined Manny on the blanket. It was time for introductions. Manny beamed about his longtime friendship with Noah and gave an overview of his strengths as a leader. He then spoke about Linda's great business acumen and how grateful he was for her presence in the pod. "I've been eager to get us all together because we share the same longing. We're longing to see our companies transformed into something new. We're committed to being broken in as leaders. We're intentionally making Life happen in our workplaces with confident humility, but unfortunately, the world doesn't always make it easy for us, so we need each other for support and encouragement."

Noah chimed in, "Manny and I have been getting together every week to encourage each other and learn about Life.

We thought it was time to invite some other broken-in folks who want to see Life flowing through their organizations too."

Linda had heard all this from Manny before, but hearing someone else say it somehow made the whole quest for Life at work seem bigger and more real. Linda smiled. "I'm honored to be here."

Manny jumped in. "If we learn from each other's successes and mistakes, we'll all get better at the basics of leadership much faster."

"Well count me in, gentlemen," Linda said. "Are you planning to meet up once a week?"

Noah scooted forward to make himself comfortable. "That would be great. Maybe we could meet for lunch on Fridays since you guys are usually in town then." Manny and Linda nodded. "So Manny, what's the topic of the day?"

"Well, I wanted to talk about the location of Life. In other words, when a leader makes Life happen, where exactly does that Life show up?"

"In your people," Linda said.

"Absolutely, but if a leader does a good job, Life also shows up in another place as well. There are always multiple bottom lines. When you're leading, you're achieving a mission through human assistants. So the two realms of Life you're being trusted with are the mission and the human assistants.

"Your mission represents the Life of all your company's stakeholders. For example, when the Blue Pod completes an assignment well, we facilitate Life for that client's employees, customers and the wider community. We also generate profits for Cyrus & Hopkins, which helps to make Life possible for the firm's partners and employees. Your job as a leader is to make Life happen for your customers, your colleagues, your investors, your vendors and your community too. You do that primarily by making sure your team accomplishes its mission well. I know this sounds so obvious, but you'd be surprised how often leaders neglect one realm of Life or the other."

A flying insect had been buzzing around Manny's head a few times and it finally landed on his ear. Manny swatted furiously at it. Noah and Linda didn't try too hard to stifle their laughter.

He went on. "The notion of keeping an eye on both realms is a practice I picked up from home. If you're a good parent, you want more than just good relationships with your children; you're also on a mission to get results. You expect your kids to get good grades in school, perform their chores well and practice good manners at the dinner table. In other words, parents want their kids to be happy *and* to produce results. They want to see Life happen in those two ways. The same holds true at work."

Linda searched the treetops as if she'd find inspiration there. "That's good. This whole Life approach isn't just some feel-good way to celebrate 'nice' leaders and defend their poor performance. A leader can't focus on his people alone. Results aren't optional at work. You know what I mean?" She looked at both men. "Focusing on the missional realm of Life is what keeps 'nice' leaders in line. It's what makes them effective in the real world and reminds them that Life is not for wimps."

Manny finished a sip from his water bottle and agreed. "You're right. Life demands results. In business we constantly focus on making results happen, but most of us don't bother to measure the actual Life produced by our missions to provide goods and services. We really should because you get whatever you measure. Different teams, of course, measure results in different ways. A successful mission could be measured by the number of new customers acquired, the beauty of artwork produced or the dependability of information technology. And for each of those missions, you need to be accountable to Life. After all, what's the use of getting new customer orders unless they further the Life of your customers? What good is art unless it helps people experience Life? What good is IT unless it advances the Life of the business processes it serves? If your mission hasn't produced much Life, your organization is pretty worthless."

Noah asked, "Want to tell her how you became so passionate about remembering both realms of Life?"

"What?"

"Tell her how you became so passionate about this."

"What?"

Noah shook his head and chuckled. He turned to Linda. "Manny used to work at a bank. When he got into his first leadership position there, it became clear that he cared for his people, but he was afraid of confronting them. He avoided confrontation like the plague. He hardly corrected his staff. No matter how abysmal things got with their performance, he never placed them on probation or fired them."

Manny joined the audible world again, tag-teaming with Noah by saying, "Since I failed to correct the underperformance I saw, I was unwittingly rewarding it. I was avoiding confrontation at the expense of my mission's success. Then when the strongest workers on my team saw the slackers coasting by without any correction, they got discouraged because they realized I wasn't appreciating the value of their hard work. Needless to say, my boss reprimanded me. But what stung me even more was that one of my best workers let me know that I had really disappointed him because I'd fallen asleep at the wheel."

Noah put his hand on Manny's shoulder. "Those were some hard times, but you finally made it through."

"Things got better once I stopped trying to be seen as a nice leader and I started making sure I was breathing Life into my people *and* my mission. I learned how to honor my people, even when I had to discipline them. The more I kept my eyes on both realms of Life, the more my people respected me as a leader.

In time, they really invested themselves in achieving the missions I set before them."

"Interesting." Linda blinked in surprise. "All of my old bosses actually had the opposite problem. They focused on results like crazy but forgot to focus on their people. They extracted all the results humanly possible from me, but they never recognized my humanity in the process. They demanded results at the expense of my Life. My colleagues and I felt like we were slowly dying. Obviously, bad things happen when a leader forgets either realm."

"Good point."

Her eyebrow ruffled as she formed a question. "So how do you handle things when you have to choose between the needs of your people and your mission?"

Noah went first. "Great question. Leaders tend to jump too quickly to the conclusion that either their people or projects have to suffer. But for the most part, Life isn't some zero-sum game where you can only succeed in your mission at the expense of your people or vice versa. I'd say that about ninety-five percent of the time, if you're willing to be resourceful, the pressure can push you to discover a creative way to make Life happen for both your mission and your people.

"For example, I once managed a difficult position that had a high turnover rate. The job had to be done, but whoever I hired for the position was doomed to suffer from burnout. After applying some creative thought to the situation, I came up with a Life-giving solution that honored my people and the mission as well. I implemented a work-sharing system so that everybody on our team did the dreaded job for a short time on a rotating basis. Now our mission is thriving and no one's burnt out." He looked over toward Manny. "Tell her about Aiden. That's a good example of balancing the two realms."

"Sure." Manny turned to Linda. "I used to be a vice president in a telecom company in Kansas City. One of my direct reports, Aiden, was performing poorly shortly after I hired him. I took him aside privately and confronted him about the problem. He acknowledged the situation and said that he would improve. A month later, it was clear that Aiden couldn't turn the situation around by himself, so I had a follow-up conversation with him and made arrangements for him to attend a training course to correct his deficiency. I also asked Samantha, one of my other direct reports, to get together with him twice a week to mentor him in the underperforming area."

Noah interrupted. "I'd like to point out that Manny was employing his home Life skills at work. He modeled confident humility by not giving up on Aiden at the first sight of trouble. He engaged Aiden in Life-giving conversations. He provided training and mentoring to show Aiden that he was important to the team and to give him a chance at success."

Manny smiled. "Tell me again how much I pay you to be my promoter? At any rate, Aiden's performance had improved only negligibly by the three-month mark. It was clear to me that he didn't have the ability to meet the performance targets I'd set for him. It's fine to make mistakes, but it's not alright to repeat the same mistake forever. So, I relieved Aiden of his position. Since there was no other suitable position for him in the company, I made sure he got a decent severance package so his family could have income until he found a new job. Finally, I hired a new, more competent executive to fill his place on the team."

"Perfect example," Noah cut in again. Linda was enjoying the way that Noah and Manny flowed together in conversation. When one interrupted the other, no one's pride was hurt. It was all okay. "That was a perfect example of a time when it may have seemed like Manny was forced to choose between harming a person or the mission, but honestly, he did a great job making Life happen in both realms. Some people would argue that firing someone can't be Life-giving at all, but it sure can be if you do it the right way and for the right reasons."

"Exactly," said Manny. "At the three-month point, I decided that the price of giving Aiden Life at work became too costly to the Life of the mission and the company's stakeholders. I had to have faith that Aiden would find Life elsewhere. Our operations were suffering, and as the leader, I had to make a call. It wasn't easy, but it had to be done. By protecting the integrity of my mission, I protected the Life of my customers and all the stakeholders under my company's care. And the morale of my team improved too."

Noah added, "But you also let Aiden go in a way that helped him to understand that he was important and worth fighting for. And your severance package also helped to ease his transition into a new job. No more demoralizing days at work for Aiden. No more dreading the fact that he wasn't measuring up to his mission. That's a valid way to make Life happen. You were freeing Aiden to move on to another job where he could successfully contribute his talents and create results."

Linda chuckled. "Making Life happen ain't for the faint of heart. I'll say it again, sometimes there's a difference between Life and 'nice.' Leaders who try to be nice all the time can't accomplish their mission well through their people." Linda had been taking notes the whole time so she could transcribe them to her laptop later.

- **Life is not for wimps. Life demands results from leaders in two realms: the Life of the people on your team, and the Life produced when your team achieves its mission well. Your team's mission represents the Life of your stakeholders, including your customers, colleagues, bosses, investors, vendors and community.**
- **A leader has to make sure that Life is showing up in <u>both</u> realms at all times by using confident humility.**

- **Keeping your eyes on both realms of Life may seem like an obvious priority, but you'd be surprised how often leaders neglect one realm or the other. Neglecting either one will have serious consequences for your stake-holders.**
- **Don't give in to believing that you're forced to harm either your people or your results. When you learn how to lead creatively, very rarely will you be forced to choose between your people and your mission. This is why it's so important for us to be broken in. We need to discover the ways that Life can show up in both realms.**

A gust of wind prompted the trees to sing and dance in undulating waves. It caught the three by surprise. Noah took in the breeze. Linda stretched her back. Manny took another sip of water and continued the discussion. "Lots of companies have over-focused on efficiency to the point where they've artificially separated the rational from the relational. They made us believe we have to choose between having efficiency and having meaningful relationships. We've been brainwashed. We've learned to compartmentalize our lives into the rational work compartment and the relational home compartment. But the truth is that there's only one compartment—"

"The 'Your Life' compartment," Noah interjected.

"Exactly. Work is just one of the ingredients that make up your Life. A good leader knows this. This knowledge is the reason why a broken-in leader can produce so much greater results than other leaders do. When you lead with confident humility, you're acknowledging someone's whole Life by inspiring efficiency from them in a way that their hearts and minds can sustain forever."

In the midst of Manny's passionate remarks, an unexpected and sober look washed over his face. He met Linda's eyes.

"So many organizations have focused on achieving missional results at the expense of their people. This unbalanced way of doing things came about because of discrimination against women in the workplace."

He turned to Noah. "A lot of guys are skilled at maintaining solid relationships." He looked back at Linda. "But in my own experience, I've found more women than men who regularly sacrifice to invest in relationships. Obviously, the most balanced and effective companies are the ones that have a good blend of female and male leaders. So, when an organization lacks the presence of strong, feminine leaders, its corporate culture can end up lacking the Life-giving relational priorities that women have to offer. Then both men and women workers end up lacking the fullness of Life they deserve at work."

He paused for a moment before continuing. "Linda, you've had bosses who've simply used you for results for many years. I'm sorry. What your bosses did was wrong. You deserved better." Manny looked directly at her. "Will you accept my apology on behalf of all the professional jerks who distorted your Life over the years?"

There was a blank look on Linda's face. An apology was the last thing she expected. She smiled and had no words to express more than "Thank you." Thoughts and emotions were swirling. Years worth of vindication was stirring within. She felt an inner healing taking place that she never knew she needed.

The three discreetly wiped their eyes as they stood up. They descended from the rock. After they passed through the park gate, they hugged each other. Noah walked off in his direction while Linda and Manny headed in theirs.

While waiting for the elevator, Linda finally spoke again, saying, "I really like Noah. The same confident humility I see in you is in him as well." The elevator arrived and they stepped in. "We all got so caught up in discussing the good stuff that I forgot to ask him what he did for a living."

Manny pressed the button marked "25." He looked up at the floor readout display and smiled. "He's a janitor."

Linda's eyes dilated in disbelief. "Are you kidding me?"

"No, it's true. Noah works for a high school as their head janitor. Three guys report to him and he runs the most gleaming, spotless high school in the entire city. He spends a good deal of time befriending and mentoring the students there. Over the years, he's helped two teenagers avoid suicide and helped countless others overcome obstacles to Life."

Linda was again speechless.

The doors opened and they stepped into the Cyrus & Hopkins reception area. Manny pulled the mobile phone out of his pocket as they walked down the hallway. "Let me double check the time of this morning's pod meeting." He was about to pull up his schedule on the phone when he stopped walking. "Wait a sec, I have a text message." Linda stopped too.

Jack's message was succinct:

You went too far.

The associates must stop ALL work for Osanto's effective immediately if they want to keep their jobs.

I'll deal with you when I return.

Right there in the hallway, Linda heard something unexpected.

"Shit!" Manny exclaimed under his breath. He looked up at Linda. "Sorry."

She laughed. "No problem. It's actually comforting to know you're human."

Manny shook his head and handed over his phone. She read the message and gasped. He started patting his hands against the side of his pants.

❖   ❖   ❖

CHAPTER EIGHTEEN

The associates filed into Conference Room B for the 10:30 pod meeting. Linda was still recovering from her time in the park, but she was also wondering how long it would be until she heard news about the Green Pod position. On top of that, she was really curious to find out how the drama with Jack and Osanto's would pan out.

Adam wandered over to the water table and put down the box of donuts he'd brought for the team. He asked, "Anybody want some water?" over his shoulder. He had a few takers so he filled up glasses and served them.

Manny stood in the hallway just outside the conference room, talking with Rachel. Actually, Rachel was doing all the talking. She was listing the benefits of her new software system or something. Manny wasn't really listening. His mind was on his associates: how blessed he was to have them, how much he didn't want them to lose their jobs. He surprised himself as he realized how much he'd grown to care for each of them—and not just because they were high performers. A few times during the conversation with Rachel, he stole a glance though the open doorway to the conference room. The koosh balls were out and he glimpsed Lee throwing one at Linda's right shoulder for fun.

She awoke from a daydream and reciprocated. Lee ducked and the koosh hit Adam instead. Manny chuckled, causing Rachel to wrinkle her face in confusion. "Something funny?" she asked. "Sorry," he replied, walking through the doorway. "I've got to get this meeting started." Linda threw a koosh ball at Manny and it bounced squarely off his forehead. He flashed a mischievous smile, as if her comeuppance were sure to come. His smile soon faded as he remembered the occasion for the meeting. "Houston, we have a problem." He dropped the Osanto's file on the table with a thud. The room quieted down.

"Guys, our situation is changing. I want to let you know what's going on." He sighed. "Jack sent a text message making it clear that you have to stop all work for Osanto's immediately if you want to keep your jobs." Lee and Adam looked at each other in disbelief. The rest of the pod had their eyes riveted on Manny. Jack had threatened the associates' job security before. The pod had typically written off his remarks as harmless invective. Nevertheless his latest threat managed to arouse a measure of fear in their hearts.

Manny continued, "I've tried to contact him but his phone's turned off. He's angry because he didn't expect us to log so many hours on Osanto's. We've all known from the start that Jack wasn't excited about this project, but I want you to recall that I led this assignment only after Jack gave me permission." Manny strolled around the room with his hands clasped behind his back as he sometimes did. "Anyhow, it shouldn't come as a surprise that Jack is scared, because he doesn't know about the real success we've accomplished in this short time. He doesn't know that Ricky has asked us to put the business plan together for Osanto's Express. He's not aware that we haven't neglected any of our other assignments. In fact, since we're waiting for crucial information to come from two other clients, we're at a standstill with those projects through no fault of our own. Once Jack discovers how much our pod has done for Osanto's and how close we are to getting the national contract, I'm sure he'll overcome his fear. He'll come on board with us and Deborah Hopkins. We all want the national contract."

Manny sat down at the head of the table. "So friends, I leave it up to you. I'm headed to Osanto's this afternoon to help write the business plan. I'm not leaving Ricky high and dry now. If any of you still want to come, I'll be glad to have you. If not, I won't think any less of you."

Adam looked to his left and right, gauging the temperature of his colleagues before he spoke up. "I think I speak for all of us when I say, 'We're with you, Coach.'" Turning to his fellow associates he then took a poll. "All in favor of continuing with Osanto's please indicate your intent by koosh ball." Two seconds later, Manny almost fell backwards out of his chair as a hailstorm of eight koosh balls overwhelmed him at top speed.

The pod had spoken. Over time, they had been measuring Manny's character and contrasting it with Jack's. They had faith that all would somehow work out fine if they just followed Manny's lead. Besides, they had no aspirations of quitting the project when major success seemed so close at hand. It also helped to know that Jack could never fire all the associates together, especially with Deborah Hopkins so interested in Osanto's.

Manny felt humbled and anxious at the same time— humbled as the pod delivered its vote of confidence in his leadership, anxious at the thought of Jack returning. Would Manny even have a job tomorrow? More important, did he do the right thing by overriding Jack's instructions and rallying the pod for the Osanto's trip?

Later that morning Linda sat in a different conference room and finally heard the words she had prayed for. They hung there in the air long after they were spoken. "Congratulations, Linda, you've got the promotion," said Deborah Hopkins. The partners of the Hiring and Promotions Committee added their heartfelt applause. Linda's face was radiant. Ira, one of the partners, motioned for Linda to address the group. She got up from her chair on the side of the room and walked to the head of the conference table. Deborah smiled, shook Linda's hand and said, "Committee, allow me to introduce Ms. Linda Flores, the next manager of the Green Pod." Another round of hearty applause ensued.

Linda had pictured this moment in her mind many times. It seemed surreal now. "I want to thank you all so much for this vote of confidence. It's a huge honor to be chosen. I've been waiting a long time for this moment." She paused and looked around the table. She inhaled before continuing. "Which is why it's so hard for me to believe what I'm about to say."

Silence enveloped the room. The thought of Mallory, the broken-in softball player, ran through Linda's mind and she smiled. Tears welled up in her eyes. "As much as I truly, truly desire this opportunity, I believe that Bernadette Waters would actually be a better choice for the position."

The partners shifted in their seats and glanced at each other. Pages ruffled. Someone coughed. Linda looked directly at the partners and continued, "The trend is clear: many of the new clients we're targeting will be needing IT help from us. We need to strengthen our capability in technology consulting. In this recession, it's the one area where we're seeing an increase in demand. We all know that the Green Pod is the one group in our firm with the best shot at developing our reputation in this area. Now, while I'm good at IT strategy, Bernadette is absolutely great. While I might be able to bring in one or two new tech-based projects over the next year, she could probably land three or four. We need to gain a foothold in this sector to compete against other firms. So while I would love to accept this position,

I must decline the offer and ask you to please reconsider in favor of Bernadette." With that Linda walked back to her seat.

The partners looked on in disbelief. An eternity passed with no one speaking. Nobody could deny that it was a brave thing to say, but given the cutthroat spirit of competition that typically prevailed at the firm, the partners struggled to decide whether Linda was the wisest or most brainless consultant they'd ever encountered. They worked hastily to construct a mental grid to understand Linda's choice. They searched the far corners of their minds for some ulterior political motive they could assign to her action, but they could find nothing that would stick. It seemed she was truly being transparent; she actually cared for the mission of the firm more than she cared about being promoted.

The "wow" that Deborah had been repressing finally fell out of her mouth, followed by, "Thank you, Linda. Obviously... umm." She chuckled. "Obviously, you caught us by surprise. One never quite knows what to expect with you Blue Pod people." The room erupted in nervous laughter. Deborah laughed again and then put on the serious face of a managing partner. She cleared her throat and attempted to regain a tone of normalcy. "We're obviously going to have to discuss this matter further as a committee, so... um, give us a chance to meet again and we'll be in touch with you." Linda nodded. "So what's next on the agenda. Ah yes." And the topic was changed.

Linda wasn't sure, but for a second she thought she detected a faint look of envy on Deborah's face.

Linda picked up her purse and walked toward the door. For the entire meeting, she had purposely avoided visual contact with Manny, who had been sitting in the back of the room. She feared that if she looked at him, even for a second, she would lose her composure in front of the partners. At last she looked. A wave of gratefulness overwhelmed her as she saw Immanuel K. Johnson staring back at her with tears in his eyes and a smile on his face. He was clearly proud of her. She was proud of herself too.

He approached her. "That was the bravest thing I've ever seen done at this firm," he said, holding the door open for her to leave the room. "It was epic."

"I have to admit, that's the bravest thing I've ever done," she said as they walked down the hallway.

"Mark my words. Your investment will have an impact on Life around here. It has to."

A few minutes later, Linda finished adjusting her hair and freshening her makeup in the mirror. She walked out of the ladies' room and down the corridor. Lee and Adam were hovering around the doorway to her office.

"Is it true?" Lee asked.

"What happened in there?" Adam exclaimed at the same time.

Linda laughed out loud. "The grapevine doesn't take long around here."

Rachel leaned her head over to the far side of her desk so she could hear what was going on. Lee whispered, "One minute we heard that you were promoted. The next minute we heard you turned it down. What happened?"

Linda waved the guys into her office and shut the door. She sat on top of her desk and they slid into the seats in front of her. She giggled because it was one of those weird moments you see in the movies. Lee and Adam were perched on the edge of their seats, wide-eyed in amazement, eagerly waiting to hear the truth. Linda could tell that Life was about to flow through her, just like it had through Mallory the softball player. Life was about to consume other people too. Linda had paid the price earlier, confidently and humbly, and now Life was going to multiply. Somehow she just knew this. Her sacrifice would have its impact. It had to. And now telling the story was just the next logical step to help Life show up the way it wanted to all along. So be it.

"It's true. They offered me the position I was dreaming of and I turned it down." She saw the confused faces she expected to see.

"Early this morning, I was sitting in my apartment trying to figure out why I was feeling uncomfortable. Of course, the first thing that came to mind was, you know, I guess I'm feeling nervous since I really want the position and they might give it to Bernadette today. But as I sat there, just checking in with myself, I realized that that wasn't it. The feeling was actually my intuition confirming that Bernadette was indeed the best candidate for the job. She rocks in the IT world and the Green Pod really needs that advantage more than they need to have me. That cautionary feeling was my conscience telling me not to steamroll over Bernadette." She didn't say it to the guys, but she knew that intuition was the voice of Life.

Lee said, "I'm so in awe of you. This sounds just like something Manny would do. Did he put you up to this?"

She shook her head. "No. This was my decision. But Manny's done a lot to bring me to this point of clarity. For instance, I tried a way of making decisions that Manny taught me. First, I took some time to discover how Life wanted to show up. I recognized that the overall Life of the firm needed Bernadette's IT skills and industry connections. I also acknowledged that my Life counted just as much as Bernadette's and that the pod needed my style of leadership too. And as I was considering all these things, I was astonished to find I didn't need to become a manager to thrive. I only needed to know that I had what it took to be a great manager. Because I was confident that I deserved the promotion, I was able to give it away for a greater good. I didn't have anything left to prove to myself. My needs were taken care of, so I could afford to focus on making Life happen for the firm."

Adam shook his head. "I hear what you're saying, but I'm a little sad. I really wanted you to get that promotion."

"Thanks, Adam. I know. And I have faith that my day is still coming. I'll be promoted then and the circumstances I step into will be right for me and no one else."

Lee piped up. "Was there a next step for you this morning after you discovered how Life wanted to show up?"

"The next step was to invent an action plan to make that Life happen for the firm. So I brainstormed on my couch and finally recognized that the best option looked like me talking to the committee to clear the way for Bernadette. The final step was just to do it with confidence and humility."

"You sound like Coach," Adam laughed out.

Linda studied Adam's face for signs of ridicule, but she found the presence of sincere respect instead. She saw the same in Lee. "Thank you both."

Lee was fiddling with the arm of his chair. "I know this might sound weird, but I'm proud of you, Linda. You've grown so much over the last months. You're a different person. You're fearless."

She smiled. "I'm not fearless yet, but I'm working on it." Linda tucked a lock of hair behind her ear. "You guys should definitely come this Friday to a brown-bag discussion that Manny and his friend Noah are starting if you want to learn more. But for now I'll say this: if you want to know how to grow in confident humility, look for examples of people who lead in ways that are untainted by self-interest. Look at Manny. Look at how good families interact. It's happening around you all the time. It's not that hard. It's just that we're not used to bringing all of the good stuff from home to work yet. But that's changing."

"You pay attention to what goes on in homes?" Adam queried.

"Absolutely. I did my part today in leading the firm and the Green Pod. I made space available for good things to happen. But really all I did was what my mama did long ago for my sister and me. Mama sacrificed and made space for us to grow so we could thrive. I'm telling you, families are where it's at."

"I believe you." Adam stood up. "I have to grab my stuff from my office before we head over to Osanto's." Lee got up too. They praised Linda again for her bravery and walked out of the office. Linda sat down in her chair, pulled up the Leadership Lessons document on her computer and keyed in a few notes:

- **Every time you act with confident humility, you make an impact. Life always flows from confident and humble leadership.**
- **I never knew that leading by making Life happen for other people could make me feel so alive! This is what I was born for. Mama would be proud!**

Linda held her head in her hand and reflected. That day would mark a turning point; it was the moment when she knew that Life was truly established within her.

An hour later, the express train to Stamford was hurtling down the track somewhere in Connecticut. Instead of sitting in a commuter railcar seat, Linda might as well have been sitting on a throne surrounded by her royal court. Tom, Lee, Adam, Manny, and everyone else found a spot near the queen and listened to more of the story. They opened their hearts and minds to the brilliance of the most counterintuitive action ever taken in the history of Cyrus & Hopkins.

Who could have guessed what would happen in the weeks that followed? Who could have known that Linda's example would have the effect of a nuclear bomb, obliterating all fellow associates' inclinations to indulge in professional vanity? Just try to grandstand and four or five associates would chew your head off. Office politics within the Blue Pod? Not likely. How could you maneuver for personal advantage when you'd be hurting people like Linda and Manny who were at your side, ready to sacrifice themselves for you? How could you only talk about the weather and sports when people were sharing their dreams with you?

In some ways, the pod would begin to feel like another organization—like a family.

❖   ❖   ❖

CHAPTER NINETEEN

I t was around seven o'clock that evening. Manny was back in New York and dead tired after spending an afternoon hard at work in Connecticut. He was stepping over puddles on the sidewalk on 57th Street. The air was still damp from the earlier rain. He kept a good distance from the curb, avoiding the spray of the passing cars. He turned the corner and saw the concrete and glass building that held Cyrus & Hopkins. Even though it was late, he wanted to finish up some paperwork in the office. The rest of the pod had gone to their homes already. They had successfully assisted the Osanto's team in fleshing out about a third of their business plan. Ricky was pleased as could be. There were even initial signs of trust resurfacing in Sarah Hunter and the task force.

Manny hoisted his bag on his shoulder and pushed through the revolving door. Halfway through the circle, he made out a familiar figure standing inside the lobby. Jack was back. His tall, lanky frame was leaning against the security desk and his arms were folded. A wave of fear radiated outward from Manny's gut. The knot in his stomach took less than two seconds to form. His heartbeat rose.

Manny came out of the swinging doors. "Hi, Jack." Manny kicked himself mentally for overplaying the friendliness in the tone of his greeting. He was shooting for something in between overly eager and too aloof. Jack just smiled in response. They stared at each other. Manny wondered whether Jack could hear his heart beating too.

Jack spoke. "Shall we take a walk?" He gestured toward the revolving door. A walk with Jack was the last thing Manny felt like doing, but he knew he had to.

They went through the doors and headed toward the store-fronts on 57th Street. Two long blocks and not a word was shared. Manny stopped abruptly in front of a furniture store. A few paces later, Jack turned around.

Hordes of concerns flooded Manny's head: is Jack about to make me look like an insubordinate idiot in front of the pod and Deborah Hopkins? Is he going to have a real conversation with me for once or will he just fire me? How will I take care of Susan and the kids without this job? Did I do right by going back to Osanto's?

"Jack, what's going on here?" Manny finally said. "We used to be good friends and now there's no trust, no communication. What are you so mad about?"

Jack was wearing a hurt and perplexed look. It was the first sign of authenticity that Manny had seen in Jack for a long time. Manny took a step closer but Jack raised his hand like a policeman to halt traffic. "Pay attention, Johnson. My father was a CEO. My brother runs half of Wall Street and I paid my dues to become one of the world's leading consultants. My father raised us to know business inside and out. I've spent decades building my career and I finally made partner. I made it to this point and then I made the mistake of hiring you to be my right-hand man. I left the office for one week and you led the pod in a revolution against me."

Manny tried to interrupt, but Jack raised his hand again to silence him. "Keep listening, Manny. It's time you started listening to what I say." Jack circled around Manny slowly. "You stole the hearts of my associates and now you're going after the glory too. If I were an associate, I'd probably choose you instead of me too. You've beguiled everybody."

Manny took a chance and interrupted. "Jack, the pod respects you—"

Jack was seething. "Tell me, should I rely on your comforting words or the truth? The truth is that you have more influence over the pod than I do and that's a problem. I'm the partner but they're following the manager. They turned out to be ungrateful sons of—"

"Well, I'm glad you're talking with me first before you speak to the pod, because the crap coming out of your mouth right now is what makes people disconnect from you. If you want to know how to reconnect and lead better, I can help you with that. That's my job and that's my privilege because I'm your friend. But stop pretending that you have no clue why the pod is so distant with you. You've projected this aura of elitism and invulnerability instead of giving us a living, breathing person. You haven't cared to become the leader we all need. You haven't wanted it enough. Now, when I've been in front of the pod, I've been trying to present you and your decisions in the best light possible—"

"Don't give me that!" Jack walked off. "You've been scheming the whole time, trying to take my place. I never gave you permission to take the whole pod to Osanto's."

Manny caught up to him. "No, but you said I could use volunteers, and that's all I did. I didn't coerce anyone to sign up. You accuse me of trying to take your place. Exactly when did this happen? When was I being selfish? Give me one example! Give me just one time when I tried to damage your interests or turn someone away from you." They stopped and he was facing Jack squarely now. "What if I can show you the opposite? What if I can show you how much I've been trying to support you and build you up all along? Will you admit then that I've been good for the team and for you?"

"This is pointless." Three large garbage trucks thundered down the street, making it pointless to talk indeed. The two men stared each other down, waiting for the trucks' roar to subside.

A family of Japanese tourists shuffled past. Manny stepped aside to make room for them, then stepped back into place. "Didn't you bring me from Kansas City to help you lead the team?" Jack returned a stare that showed just how little he cared to answer a rhetorical question. "Well, did I accomplish that mission or not? The team is working better than ever before. Check! Our projects are running more smoothly than ever. Check! The days of high employee turnover have gone. Check! In fact, people in other pods now want to transfer into the Blue Pod because they can tell that we've got something good. Am I making this up or is it true?"

Jack stepped in closer to make a point. "It's true, but you did it to create your own empire rather than to build mine." He paused for a moment, looking directly into Manny's eyes. "Where did you take the pod this afternoon?" He asked the question in an eerily innocent-sounding tone.

Manny looked at the sidewalk. A wet blanket of guilt kept him from lifting his head. He spluttered something in a low voice.

"I didn't hear you."

Manny looked up. "We went to Osanto's. I promised Ricky we'd go before I got your text message. No other client projects suffered."

"Didn't I explicitly instruct you to stop all work for Osanto's?"

Manny tried to sound as if his conscience were clear. "Yes."

"Didn't I warn you of the repercussions of anyone who disobeyed my instructions?"

"You wouldn't return my calls even though—"

Jack shouted, "That's not the point!" He turned to walk away again but returned instantly. "I gave you clear instructions and you ignored me. You led the entire pod to do the exact opposite of what I told you to do. Are these the actions of a loyal manager? You totally undermined me and caused the insubordination of all the associates. You want an example of how you've been building your empire at the expense of mine? Well there you go. It's not hard to see whose agenda you followed today."

Where were the supposed crowds of New York City? The sidewalk seemed as desolate as a ghost town. Manny opened his mouth to speak but Jack's arm again sliced through the air dangerously close to his face. A raging fire was burning behind Jack's eyes. Manny caught a glimpse of it briefly before looking down at the sidewalk again. This was torture.

Jack exhaled deeply. His voice took on a surprisingly wistful tone. "Back in high school, did you ever bring a girl to the dance? You're nervous as hell because you don't know if she really likes you, but she says yes. Then at the dance, some other guy comes and grabs her for the first dance. When she comes back, she's polite with you, but she still has stars in her eyes from the first dance. She dances with you but she's dreaming of the other guy."

Manny sat down on the steps in front of the furniture store. His brain was fried. His conscience was tired. Everything was becoming fuzzy.

Jack went on. "What you've been doing at Osanto's may be great for your career but don't try to make it seem like you've done it for me. Don't play it off like I should be grateful. You betrayed me. When I hear the word Osanto's, I want to vomit. You've accomplished a lot with the pod but I haven't been a part of the success. I was supposed to be a part of it."

Manny sighed. His conscience was pierced. He couldn't hold the apology back any longer. "I should have stopped the project when you told me. I'm sorry." Jack sat down on the steps too. "I got so carried away by a desire to see things through that

I stuck my fingers in my ears. I pretended not to hear you."
Manny shook his head as he said, "I was wrong."

They spent a few minutes just looking out at the sidewalk.
A couple of young ladies in eveningwear sauntered by with
Jimmy Choo shoes and Prada purses, talking about someone's
sadly lacking Facebook page. A few taxis zoomed toward the
Eastside. A bus picked up a lone passenger across the street and
headed west.

Manny searched his memory and realized that he'd been oper-
ating as if his own magnificence required Jack to be neutralized.
He'd inadvertently let fear and selfishness cloud his judgment.
Fear and pride—the opposite of confidence and humility.

"Manny, you let me down."

"I know. I can see why you feel betrayed." At that point, an
idea came to Manny's mind. It was a way that Manny could have
done things differently to make more Life happen. "I should
have called Ricky and told him that we couldn't come today
because an urgent situation came up at work." This scenario
would have allowed Manny to respect Jack's wishes and save face
with Osanto's as well. After all, Jack's text message definitely
qualified as urgent. "That would have been the right thing to do."

Jack's poker face remained.

"Look, Jack, you're the only partner that the Blue Pod has.
What you say goes. I want you to know I intend to keep my
ambition in check when it goes against your instructions from
now on." Manny swallowed and took a deep breath. Then he
took a chance. "So will you forgive me?"

Jack snorted a chuckle. "Will I forgive you? Who says that?"
Then he turned and saw sincerity in Manny's eyes. Jack stood up,
scratched his head and exhaled. Manny looked up, obviously
waiting for a response. None came. Jack shook his head and
walked off in the direction of the office.

In Manny's estimation, when Jack shook his head, he was
communicating "I don't know" or "I have nothing to say." Manny

was about ninety percent certain. But the ten percent weighed heavily on him.

It took about ten minutes for Manny to pull himself off the damp steps of the furniture store. He wandered east along the 57th Street storefronts in a daze. What had just happened? He didn't even know if he was still employed.

He stopped on the corner of Madison Avenue by the Q32 bus stop. Every now and then he took the bus home instead of the subway; it took longer but was more enjoyable. Manny was in no rush to go home that night. He had no idea what to say to Susan.

An elderly woman with a Bloomingdale's shopping bag was waiting at the stop. They exchanged smiles briefly. The bus took only three or four minutes to come. He boarded after the woman and found a seat near the front. He leaned his head against the window as the blocks rolled by. He noticed a mother with a child in a stroller get on the bus at Second Avenue. He walked to the back of the bus so they could sit together near the front door.

The bus climbed over the East River on the 59th Street Bridge. Manny was hanging on to the metal bar overhead. His eyes panned the shimmering skyline of Manhattan.

The bus was soon meandering through traffic on Queens Boulevard. Manny hopped off in front of the White Castle restaurant on 43rd Street. He walked a few blocks north into the heart of Sunnyside Gardens, still wondering what he was going to say to Susan.

He reached his red brick house and opened the front door. He was immediately bowled over by Ryan and Samantha who had been waiting for him to come home. Their giggles and stories about school made Manny forget his woes temporarily. When Susan asked Manny about his day, he simply replied, "Interesting. Details soon." It was understood that "soon" meant when the kids were put to bed.

He spent about twenty minutes helping Samantha with her math homework and then he helped Susan finish making dinner (salmon, chicken nuggets for the little ones, rice and broccoli). After the meal, the children wanted to watch *The Incredibles* DVD, but it was too late. Manny didn't feel badly saying "no" since they had seen the movie twice before.

Finally Samantha and Ryan were tucked into their beds with heavy eyelids. Manny brushed his teeth and then shuffled from the bathroom into his bedroom. He was wearing a tie-dyed T-shirt and plaid pajama pants. Susan was already in bed, leaning against a hill of pillows and reading a novel. She closed the book and put it on her lap as Manny entered the room. Her hair was pulled back, as it was on most nights. "So honey, what happened today? You seemed a little down when you came home."

Manny beat his pillow into shape and climbed under the sheets. He reclined on his side with his hand supporting his head, facing Susan. "It's a hard day to describe. So much happened. The good news is that Linda got the promotion and then she coura-geously gave it away to another consultant who she felt deserved it more. It was amazing. Everyone was astounded, and I know her example made a huge impact on the culture of the firm."

"And what's the bad news?"

He smiled. "Right. I forgot. You like to get the bad news first, don't you?" She smiled too. He continued, "Jack texted me and told me to stop all the pod's work on Osanto's."

"You're kidding me," she exclaimed, putting her book on the nightstand.

"And he threatened unemployment for anyone who went against his orders." Manny then squinted his eyes in disbelief over what he was about to say. "Then I made a bad judgment call. I continued working on the assignment and, after informing the pod about what Jack had said, I invited them to help me and they did."

Susan's face registered the disappointment that Manny had been dreading. The potential consequences of his bad decision were percolating through her mind. She asked, "Does Jack know? Have you talked with him yet?"

"Yeah. It was the most real conversation we've had in years. He confronted me and told me that I betrayed him. I initially tried to make him see that I've always been on his side and that he's been making things very hard for me and the pod. But I eventually realized that no matter what he's done wrong, I was wrong too. So I apologized. I asked him to forgive me." With that, Manny rolled onto his back. He released a long sigh and stared at the ceiling.

"And... did he forgive you?"

"I don't know. He just kind of shook his head as if he didn't know what to say. Then he walked away."

Silence. Manny knew that Susan was processing things in her mind. He was processing too.

"Manny."

He fixed his eyes on her and said, "Susan, I'm sorry for putting my job security in jeopardy. I got so caught up in—"

"Manny... it's okay." She took his head into her hands. "You make reckless decisions sometimes. But it's okay. You learn from them. I know your heart. I know we're going to make it somehow. Remember when we first came to New York? You were thinking about leaving the firm and then Noah encouraged you to fight. You came home that night and we discussed your staying at the firm on your own terms. I said I wanted you to live at full volume, come what may. We agreed that you would lead the pod the best way you knew how, even if it meant that you'd someday have to find a new job. Do you remember that?"

Manny nodded.

Susan rolled over into his arms, resting a hand on his chest. "Well, I still mean it. I'm not scared. Just do what's right, come what may. Make amends with Jack, but hold your head high when you see him and don't let him continue acting like an idiot. He needs to grow up."

Manny kissed her on the forehead. He liked her feisty side.

"And you know what else?" She backed up far enough to look him in the eye. "Even if you have to leave the firm, I want you to know I am the proudest wife on the planet. Manny, you always fight hard for what's right. You live a Life of sacrificial love. You're strong that way. You're strong in the right places and you're gentle in the right places too."

Now it was Manny's turn to roll into Susan. His voice was muffled because he was speaking directly into her arm, but she could still make out the words: *Thank you for your love.*

The two spent the rest of the evening in bed, discussing the pros and cons of their options if Manny were to lose his job. At 11:40, they decided they were tired. Then they prayed together, kissed goodnight and turned off the lights.

PART SIX

❖   ❖   ❖

The Aligning

CHAPTER TWENTY

The golf course was one of Connecticut's finest. The fact that it was generally impossible to get a decent tee time on a Saturday morning was no concern of Jack's. His platinum membership afforded him access to a lot of perks.

Byron Greenslate, a tall African-American man, was sitting in the passenger seat of Jack's golf cart. He was an executive vice president at Colloquium Life Insurance Company. Jack had met him earlier that week at the conference in Florida.

The cart whirred up and down green hills as it made its way toward the restaurant in the clubhouse. Jack was driving as fast as he could because both of them were hungry. The game was over. Byron had won, but he couldn't tell whether Jack had truly tried his best or whether he had just let Byron win.

Jack parked the vehicle, and a caddie, who had been riding in the back of the cart, jumped out and started putting the equipment away. Jack held the door of the restaurant open for Byron. "You've got a winning swing there, Byron."

"Thanks. I think."

The hostess seated them. Jack was confused. "What do you mean, 'you think'?"

"Well, I could tell you're pretty skillful at the game yourself. I'm just not sure you let me see all that you were capable of out there."

"Nonsense." Jack laughed. "You won fair and square. Now let's see what the special of the day is." He buried himself in the menu.

Within a few minutes, the waiter took their orders and brought them drinks. Jack took a sip and casually mentioned, "Byron, you told me back at the conference that your department might have an opportunity to expand. Why don't you tell me a little more about that?"

Byron placed the folded cloth napkin in his lap. "This is all confidential, right?"

"Absolutely."

"Good. As you probably know, Colloquium got its start selling life insurance policies to individuals. In the last few years, we've expanded into group health policies, that is, health insurance policies that we sell to companies to cover their employee groups. But we've never done life insurance for groups. It's a significant market. Take a look at these numbers." He took a pen out of his pocket, slid the paper cocktail napkin out from under his glass and scribbled a series of figures and charts onto it. He guided Jack through the business logic of the move. When the napkin got crowded, Jack took his own napkin and passed it over. Byron continued writing.

Jack's mouth was partially open. "This is brilliant. I mean, the opportunity is there. Since you're already operating in individual life and group health, your new fixed costs are almost nonexistent and your variable costs would be minimal. Your department has the marketing infrastructure and your sales force has the connections you need throughout the network. Brilliant expansion plan! You know, Cyrus & Hopkins could definitely help you with this." Jack's head was spinning. This assignment would be substantial. If the Blue Pod played its cards right, this large client might also choose the pod for future projects. Jack could taste it.

But Byron was wearing a peculiar look. Another factor was in the mix. "Yes, there certainly is a strong business argument for moving forward, and we theoretically could use your help in building a solid case for expansion and justifying it to our board—"

"But." Jack invoked the word waiting to be spoken.

Byron laughed. "But... there is a man who stands in the way. My boss Evan. He's the COO of the company and he needs to sign off on my retaining Cyrus & Hopkins. As things stand now, he seems dead-set against the idea of us expanding into any new business."

"Even if the new business is practically already your current business?"

Byron shook his head with a smile, "Jack, your problem is that you're living in the world of logic. You have to leave logic behind to some extent when you're dealing with Evan. He's one of *those* guys."

"What do you mean?"

Byron paused as the food arrived. The waiter placed a sizzling steak in front of Byron and prime rib in front of Jack. Neither touched their food.

"What I mean," Byron explained, "is that Evan's a very smart man with lots of experience in insurance, but he gets in the way of our company's success—or better said, he lets his pride get in the way of our success. He's always thinking about status. You know, if you disagree with him on something once, you forever belong to a lesser category of executive in his eyes. Unless he or one of his yes-men puts forth the proposal, the idea is never good enough. He won't listen to me. He tries to come off as friendly, but ultimately he's aloof and unapproachable. Even though I've tried for a while to put myself on his calendar, I haven't had a decent conversation with him for months."

"I'm sorry to hear that."

"He's out of touch with my department. Evan told me that the time wasn't right to chase after the group life market because we didn't have enough resources and the rewards weren't big enough to run after. So I showed him what I showed you: a way to do it with minimal costs. Then he just looked at me as if I were a child and that I'd understand one day when I grew up."

"Oh."

"Mind you, Evan's not a bad guy. He's means well, but he can't lead. And the worse part is, he won't let anyone else who's competent lead either. All the EVPs who report to Evan are waiting for him to retire so we can rescue the company. Anyhow, hopefully now you can see why I can't engage your services. I've got to do what my boss tells me, no matter how big a jerk he is."

The men dove into their platters. They were happy to have something to do with their mouths since there was not much more to say. Eventually Byron piped up, "Sorry Jack. I know that you were interested in working with us. I would have liked that. But, like I said, Evan is one of *those* guys." He looked at Jack pensively. "You know the type right?"

Jack crammed the last piece of prime rib into his mouth even though he wasn't hungry. In fact, he was feeling sick to his stomach. He had filled his mouth so that he wouldn't have to respond. He knew the type.

Susan and Manny shared a complicit smile when they heard the familiar series of thuds on Monday morning. Ryan and Samantha had finished dressing for school upstairs and were running across the floor. Manny sprinted across the living room to duck inside the coat closet. Susan approached the bottom landing as the children flew down the stairs. Samantha rested her chin on the banister. "Where's Dad?"

Susan scanned the room. Pictures of the children, friends and extended family lined the walls. The terra cotta couch had red and brown pillows strewn over it. "I don't know where Dad is, but I heard some scary noises here in the living room, almost like monster noises." She cautiously lifted up a couch cushion in search of the source of the noises.

Ryan squealed in delight. "A monstah?!!"

Samantha was peeking under the lid of the giant toy box. "It's probably Dad hiding."

"No it's not. It's a monstah," Ryan exclaimed in defiance, his smile still in place. He ran into the dining room to look under the blue tablecloth.

Samantha slowly creaked open the door of the coat closet. Susan flashed her an encouraging smile and a thumbs-up before slipping back into the kitchen to finish making lunches for school.

"Aarrrrrggghhh!" growled the monstah in a white T-shirt and plaid pajama pants. Samantha shrieked in terror as he scooped her up in his arms. Ryan screamed just as loudly even though he was clear across the room by the dining room table. He sped like a bullet across the distance into his dad's arms to join the carnage.

A few minutes later, Susan came out of the kitchen to find Manny still wrestling and tickling them both on the floor. She sighed. "Do you two have your schoolbags packed with your homework inside your bags?"

"Nooooooo," they sang in unison.

"Off you go then." She shooed them upstairs with a smile, leaving Manny sprawled flat on his back on the living room floor. He was winded from the roughhousing. She got on her hands and knees and crawled over to his side with a smile.

"Either they're getting bigger or I'm getting older," he said, making room for Susan to lay her head on his bicep.

"You may be getting bigger too," she said innocently while poking at some chub in his belly.

His voice dove an octave deeper. "Abs of steel, right there, baby. Abs of steel."

"Hey, you know what?"

"What?" he asked with an eyebrow raised.

"I'm proud of you."

Manny pulled her in close and wanted to never let go. He only loosened his grasp slightly when Ryan and Samantha bounded downstairs again and dove into the middle of their embrace. The mound of human beings on the living room carpet decided to linger, enjoying the moment. The kids would arrive at school five minutes late, but some things are worth being late for.

Rachel looked up from her computer screen and saw Manny approaching Jack's closed door. "Only a few scattered clouds," she mentioned casually.

"Good." Manny took a deep breath and knocked on the door.

He heard the muted "come in" so he opened the door and walked inside. Jack was texting on his Blackberry. Manny closed the door behind him but remained standing by the door. "Aren't you going to sit down?" Jack asked while still concentrating on his phone.

"I've been thinking a lot this weekend," Manny said.

"Good to hear."

"Jack, I really let you down."

"I heard Linda was quite the hero with Hiring and Promotions on Friday."

"I'm sorry."

"She created quite a buzz among the partners."

"Jack, I'm sorry I didn't follow your instructions."

Jack cleared his throat loudly. He pushed his chair back a few inches from his desk and crossed his legs. "Look. I'm no good at these things." He straightened the wrinkles in his shirt and centered his tie. "I, um, I forgive you."

Manny allowed himself a small smile. "Thank you." He wanted Jack to make eye contact. Eventually, he did. "Do you know that I never intended to hurt you? Not even once?"

Jack decided to stare out the window. "I know."

Manny exhaled. "Good."

"You're different than you used to be, Manny. I mean, back in B-school."

"I'm still me."

Jack turned his head back toward Manny. "What's the status of Osanto's?"

"I've stopped all the pod's work on the project. I haven't spoken to Ricky yet. Why don't I clear off the agenda for today's pod meeting. You can run the meeting. Perhaps you could listen to what the associates have to say about Osanto's. Then you could choose the best way to proceed. It'll be your call. I'll go to Ricky to explain your decision afterwards."

Jack traced his fingers against the molding on the side of the desk while he contemplated. He sighed, "Alright."

"Thank you." Manny's hand grabbed the doorknob to make his exit. He stopped in mid-twist. A powerful impulse possessed him. He was just beginning to believe that he still had a job when the impulse came to rock the boat. He released the doorknob, walked toward the desk and took a seat. Am I insane? I must be insane. I've got to say it. Don't say anything! Nevertheless, the words bolted out of his mouth, surprising both men. "Where were you when I needed you?"

Jack stared blankly.

The floodgate had been opened. "Jack, you have a problem with jealousy, and it's a deal breaker. I can't continue to work for you if every time I do something right with the pod, you take it as something wrong I'm doing to you. You've also been shutting me out of your thought process. You make it really hard for me to communicate with you. On top of that you're not attending enough pod meetings to make the associates feel like you're with them—like you're *for* them. These things take away from your effectiveness with the pod and with me. Do you understand what I'm saying?"

Ages came and went. Poker face.

Manny added, "These are the real reasons why our friendship has suffered."

Jack traced the desk molding again. Visions of an unemployment line flashed in front of Manny's eyes, but he dismissed them and a quiet confidence settled instead. He affirmed to himself that the decision to confront was a wise one, even though the stakes were high.

Jack ran his fingers through his hair and released a long groan of exasperation. He fumbled for words. "This... this is the only me I'm good at. I don't know how to change."

"Well, that's what I'm here for." Manny used a gentle voice. "I can help you, buddy. We could work together so you could become more effective with the pod. And you don't have to become someone else to be effective. But you have to want to grow as a leader. I can't do it for you. You've got to spark that desire for yourself."

"You're killing me."

Manny smiled. "I know. Just one of the perks."

Jack studied the desk molding for another moment before saying, "Go get the associates ready to present their thoughts to me on Osanto's. Just start with that, Dr. Phil."

❖   ❖   ❖

Two hours later, Jack and Manny were walking with purpose down the hallway toward Conference Room B. "Rachel, we'll be in a pod meeting," Manny said with a wink. Just before entering the room, Manny leaned over and whispered, "Remember what I mentioned about making the pod feel like you're on their side." Jack acknowledged with a nod.

The associates were seated and waiting. There was none of the usual banter going on around the conference table. Their good posture and smiling faces were an attempt to conceal the fact that they feared for their jobs. Manny sat at the side of the table, leaving the seat at the head for Jack. As Jack sat down, Linda shot Manny a glance, seeking to know if all would be okay. Manny raised his brows as if to say, we'll see.

Linda stood up before Jack could say a word to start the meeting. "Jack, we were talking about what happened. All of us…" She looked around at the table to take in the support of her fellow associates. "All of us wanted to apologize for going to Osanto's after you told us not to. We're sorry." She exhaled and sat down again.

Jack accepted the apology. "Thank you. And Linda, congratulations on your bold decision concerning the promotion you were offered. I'm glad to still have you on my team." Linda nodded. Jack then rested his elbows on the table and tented his hands. "Now it's time for me to decide what should be done with the Osanto's account. Is it a complete waste of time and energy or do we continue with it? I'm going to listen to your recommendations before I make up my mind." The room was quiet for a few seconds. Jack looked around the table. "Well, speak."

Lee jumped in. "I think Osanto's Express is an inspired plan. Adam really hit upon a powerful idea when he analyzed the market. I want to see it through to execution. But even more important, we've invested so much already and we have a big fan in Ricky. We owe it to him to finish what we started. We'll find out next week what happens with the national account."

Adam went next. "Next week is so close and the upside is so high. We'd have to be fools to drop out now, uh, respectfully."

"Thank you for your humble opinion, Adam," Manny interjected.

Over the next forty-five minutes, the rest of the associates weighed in one by one. Each of them pled for the pod to proceed full speed ahead. Some appealed to the moral responsibility the firm had to the client. Some spoke of the national account. The more they spoke, the less they worried about keeping their jobs. It was comforting to see Jack treating them all as if they were so very employed.

Manny saved the best for last. He said, "We all agree that even though the pod is busy now, we don't have a sufficient number of future projects in the pipeline. Ricky just sent me an email this morning with some new information. The scope of the national project he described is sweeping. I estimate we're talking at least $2.2 million in fees for Cyrus & Hopkins. I'd say that's worth pursuing."

Jack slapped his hand on the table, causing all heads to turn. "I've heard enough. Let's do it." The associates' eyes darted between each other.

Tom exclaimed, "If we work hard we can knock out the business plan within the week."

Jack had risen from his seat and was pacing. "Do you really think this Ricky guy will back us at the national meeting?"

Several of the associates blurted out "Yes!" "Positively," and "The guy's in love with us!"

A smile commandeered Jack's face. "Alright, let's do it." Linda, Tom and Manny spontaneously rose from their seats with a shout. Others were clapping in approval.

In the midst of the merriment, Jack called for their attention, saying, "Alright children, I mean, ladies and gentlemen. There's one last thing." The room quieted again. He turned to Manny.

"I just want to say that I regret giving the stop order for this project. You were right to bring us the Osanto's assignment in the first place."

Manny smiled. "Thanks." He then cleared his throat softly, looking at Adam.

Without missing a beat, Adam spoke, as prearranged. "Ladies and gentlemen of the Blue Pod, if you're inclined to show your loyal support for our brave leader Jack, now is the time to cast your vote of confidence by our favorite method of vote-casting."

Jack looked up and discovered an armada of koosh balls closing in at a hundred miles per hour. He lifted both arms and a leg in defense and laughed. He belly laughed. Everybody laughed. He picked a handful of koosh balls off the table and threw them back at the group. The War of the Kooshes escalated as the associates targeted each other and Manny too. Louise ran from the reception desk to see what all the hoopla was about. She was beginning to get used to the noisy Blue Pod.

❖   ❖   ❖

CHAPTER TWENTY-ONE

Lunchtime couldn't come fast enough for Lee and Adam the next Friday. Linda led them past the statue, the gates, the grass and down the road to the rock. The sun was shining. Noah waved hello and reached out his arm to help Linda up. Manny was already perched above, seated next to Daniel, a student at Columbia University. Linda sat down next to Daniel and learned that he was formerly a student at the high school where Noah worked. Noah had been mentoring him for three years now. Lucinda was new to the rock as well. She was a fashion designer who lived in Sunnyside near the Johnsons. Her kids often played with Samantha and Ryan. Keith climbed up on the rock too. He was a friend of Noah's and was a web developer with a large media conglomerate. Linda stood up to hug her friend, Cyranna, when she arrived. Cyranna was a trainer for the accounting and internal audit departments at Joval Financial Group's New York offices. Linda had met her while on the client assignment at Joval. Once all the invited people had assembled, they sat in a circle.

Noah called for everyone's attention and Manny addressed the group. "I want to thank you all for coming out today. Noah, Linda and I have been looking forward to gathering a group of friends who want to grow into better leaders. We've all been entrusted with the power and frailty of human beings to accomplish our missions. We owe it to our people and to our missions to lead skillfully. I'm going to start by giving a brief outline of our leadership approach. Don't worry if you don't catch all of the details today. We'll be here every week, sharing stories and encouraging each other, so you'll pick it up over time just by being with us."

Noah looked around in amazement at the group. Someone pinch me, he thought. Somehow he knew these people would develop into magnificent comrades who lived Life together to the fullest.

Manny continued, "The brightest stars in every field are the folks who've mastered the fundamentals. Leadership is no different. We want to get so good at the basics of good leadership that our impact overflows into our organizations and even into our city.

"So what distinguishes a breakthrough leader from a status-quo manager? Well, the difference is that the breakthrough leader has her strength under control in a way that produces Life. That difference transforms her people and energizes her team around their mission.

"The first thing we're going to do is to develop a love for Life. The foundation of good leadership is the ability to make Life happen. Life is the ultimate motive of the human race, and so the core of being a good leader is having your strength under control for the benefit of Life. Your people are always going to do whatever they think will bring them the most Life. Using that knowledge to move your venture forward is what distinguishes a wise leader from a foolish one."

Manny described Life as a person's optimal state of being and gave some examples of what Life could look like when unleashed at work. "Life is the natural overflow that happens in people when they find a meaningful purpose, connect deeply with a community, go on an adventure and make real results happen. Life is the only context that can sustain a high performance team forever. As we meet in the weeks ahead, you'll begin to understand what this 'Life' is all about and you'll discover that it's the main reason why people follow a leader." After a brief Q&A time, he said, "Let's never confuse making a living with making a Life," and he handed over the floor to Noah.

Noah shared some stories about how he targeted his fellow janitors with Life. Their lives had been transformed and his team's performance ratings had soared dramatically in the recent satisfaction surveys sent to the students, faculty and administration. Daniel shared a story about being addicted to cocaine in high school and how Noah had helped him overcome the habit. Now that Daniel was in college, Daniel had himself become a leader among his peers, constantly seeking to make Life happen for his classmates. Linda shared her story about her promotion. Adam commented on the huge impact that Linda's humble decision had made throughout the pod and the firm.

Manny added, "Whether you have a fancy title or not, when people sense that you're both tenacious and modest, it unlocks their hearts and releases them to be selfless in pursuing the team's strategy. That's how you sustain a culture of breakthroughs."

Linda wrapped things up by sharing her hope for future meetings. "Our stories about Life are powerful. Over time, we'll learn to trust each other and we'll share the stories of our successes and mistakes in trying to make Life happen. It takes courage, but I believe that each of us may be willing to be transparent with our weaknesses so that all of us can grow. We'll encourage each other and hold each other accountable to Life." She then invited everyone to come to a Fourth of July barbeque on her apartment's roof deck overlooking the harbor and fireworks.

When the hour was over, no one wanted to leave their seats, even though the "seats" were a little hard. Keith mentioned, "This is a beautiful spot, but it might be a good idea to bring some cushions next time." Everyone agreed. Manny volunteered Conference Room B as a rain location. As the people stood up,

Manny somehow knew that this diverse group would become his new family, his new comrades in the desert. He was home.

On the way down the rock, Noah again extended his hand to guide Linda. He summoned the courage to speak. "Linda, I was wondering if you might be interested in going to Shakespeare in the Park sometime. Maybe we could grab dinner first?"

Linda took a few steps on her own then accepted his hand, smiling a mischievous smile. "Noah, it almost sounds like you could be inviting me on a date."

Noah speedily reddened, the color of his face almost matching his red hair. "I didn't say it was a date… But I'm not saying it's not either." She stepped off the rock and onto the ground, letting her hand linger in his just a little longer than necessary. Manny was thrilled. He walked on, pretending not to notice. He had been encouraging Noah to take a chance, but he didn't know today would be the day his friend would strike.

One by one, the others descended. A couple of random thoughts came to Manny as he walked with the group toward the park gate. The first was about the people surrounding him. He had a feeling that everyone would eventually come to care deeply for each other. He liked that. A gathering of Life-giving market-place professionals who were on the same wavelength.

The second thought was about his brother. Caleb had always displayed so much initiative in his childhood. If he were still around, he would have been making Life happen like this too. Manny couldn't help but think that Caleb would have been proud of him. He liked that thought too.

CHAPTER TWENTY-TWO

Life at the firm of Cyrus & Hopkins LLP was never the same after those pioneering days when Manny first came to town.

Osanto's Express became a reality, with several lucrative stores located in hotspots throughout the Tri-State area. The menu was healthy and the well-pleased customers kept coming back for more. When the associates gave the final Osanto's Express presentation, Manny looked like a proud papa standing in the wings. Lee and Adam facilitated the meeting. They and the other consultants displayed passion, confidence and humility that day. They were Manny's heroes.

Ricky honored his word and lobbied hard for Cyrus & Hopkins to get the national project with Osanto Restaurants International. The firm was awarded the contract about a month after the meeting at which Jack gave his blessing for the pod to continue working. Cyrus & Hopkins would end up billing over $2.6 million in fees. Deborah Hopkins nearly had a heart attack from joy every month when she got to inspect the outgoing invoices. At one point, Ricky said, "You guys are worth every penny of it. We could make three times that amount back in the first year or two, thanks to your guidance."

The Hiring and Promotions Committee announced that Bernadette Waters would be the next manager of the Green Pod. Bernadette appeared in Linda's doorway the following day. "Linda, thank you so much. I don't even have words."

"No problem. You really deserve the position, Bernadette."

"Could I treat you to lunch someday? I'm not being as generous as I might seem by offering you lunch. I need your help. The only thing I know for sure is that leading is a lot harder than it looks when you've never led before. I've heard some incredible stories about you and the Blue Pod, and I'd love to pick your brain." Later that week they ate at the local Osanto's Bar & Grill (where else would they go?). It went well and turned into a series of lunches because Bernadette kept having more questions about leadership and Life. She soon started coming to the Friday rock gatherings as well. Life began to multiply itself through her. In time, the Green Pod became known as the second "fun pod" of the firm. Bernadette and the Green Pod were also successful in taking the firm's reputation in the field of technology consulting to the next level. Seven new technology-based assignments helped sustain the firm financially through some tough economic times that actually shut down other consulting firms that year. Linda was grateful to see all the Life she'd helped to cultivate by making space for Bernadette.

The next months saw Lee develop into an outstanding encourager. Every team has its A players and B players. Lee made sure all the B players in the pod understood their role as the much-valued bedrock of every team effort. If anyone was in a jam professionally or personally, Lee spared no expense in equipping them with the skills or help they needed. He turned into the kind of man who could walk into a room and shift the culture by his presence. Given his business acumen and his interpersonal power, it's no surprise that one day he became the CEO of a start-up software company in Austin, Texas. He led eleven employees from day one. His first task was to assemble a management team. Manny helped him with the selection process over the telephone.

Lee gave his executive team the same chance at Life that he gave the pod. The team, in turn, poured Life into the company's people, operations and brand values over the next months. Thanks to a singularly good flagship product, the company made a profit in its second year, ahead of schedule. Lee's stock options were looking pretty good.

Adam continued to grow in humility and marketing insight. In fact, he provided the winning marketing strategies needed for three projects over the next year. He asked "Coach" to set aside some time each week to mentor him in Life, and he gradually learned to provide leadership in a novel way for the firm: he began Cyrus & Hopkins's first Strategic Marketing Symposium. It started it as a bimonthly roundtable discussion for several of the firm's clients. Within six months, clients started inviting their friends from other companies. In no time, the firm became known as the go-to place for strategic marketing consulting. Adam hired an energetic staff of two to help him administer the conferences, since he spent most of his time working on client assignments with the pod. Adam got married about the same time that the symposium took off, and within a few weeks, he and his wife Wendy were expecting a child.

Although it took some time, Jack Jameson eventually surprised Manny and agreed to meet for a half-hour each week to discuss leadership. At first, it was very challenging for him to accept the fact that he wasn't good at the fundamentals of leading. A lot of the initial meetings sounded like shouting matches. However, once he was able to own his fears and pride, learning became easier. He became more and more teachable as he discovered that Manny actually wanted him to succeed.

Manny gave Jack a lot of feedback on a variety of topics: they spoke about threatening the pod's sense of job security, about not listening in general, and about barking commands instead of empowering people. They discussed the dangers of Jack potentially surrounding himself with people who only say what Jack

<u>wants to hear.</u> The two would often role-play with each other (Jack detested role-playing at first and after a few weeks learned to only mildly dislike it). During these closed-door sessions, Manny pretended to be an associate and presented Jack with a number of situations designed to show Jack how to build up people and leave space for them to grow.

Jack's handling of the pod became more constructive and encouraging as the months went by. He continued his incessant text messaging in the middle of conversations, but that was only a small detraction from the otherwise beautiful character that was emerging. One day, out of the blue, he invited Manny to go for a beer after work. They had a good time. Soon after, Jack and Manny started going to lunch regularly. Needless to say, their communication improved significantly.

Cyrus & Hopkins got a lot of positive publicity when Manny was interviewed for a *BusinessWeek* article. Deborah Hopkins nearly kissed him when she found out about the free exposure. The magazine had heard about a "revolution" going on at several organizations, including Cyrus & Hopkins. They called Manny a "statesman-executive." He spoke to the journalist about how <u>you can turn a business around by taking bold actions from a humble posture.</u> He referred to Linda's sacrifice as a watershed in the firm's history, saying, "In a competitive win-lose environment, Linda chose to neither win nor lose. She triumphed on her own terms by displacing the rat race with a system of Life… In America, many of us have lost our sense of nobility and calling as leaders. That's what people like Linda are trying to restore."

One day, about seven months after work resumed on the Osanto's project, Rachel poked her head in to Manny's office to tell him that Deborah Hopkins wanted to see him. When he arrived at her office, Jack was sitting in the discussion area with Deborah. Jack had his legs crossed and a glass of white wine in his hands. Deborah informed Manny that Jack had some news to share. Manny sat down with them.

Jack had a pleased look about him. He said, "You know how much I've always wanted to live overseas. Even when we were in business school, you remember how I dreamed of living in Asia." He uncrossed his legs and leaned forward. "Well, Deborah just offered me the chance to open up Cyrus & Hopkins's first office in Hong Kong."

After the look of shock subsided on Manny's face, he got up and hugged Jack. "Congratulations. We're going to miss you around here."

Deborah then reached out to shake Manny's hand, smiling. "Congratulations to you too." Manny stood there for a moment wondering why he was being congratulated. Deborah continued, "It seems we now have a vacant position, since the Blue Pod won't have a partner to lead it. Might you be interested?" The full partnership had unanimously authorized Deborah to extend the offer.

Manny was stupefied. Jack reached over to shake Manny's hand, but halfway through he pulled Manny in to hug him. "Congratulations, partner. And don't worry, I've already told Deborah that Linda has to be your manager. The Hiring and Promotions Committee has already cleared it."

Manny was speechless. Too much good news to internalize in such a short time. "Thank you," was all he could utter.

Deborah added, "We decided to let you have the honor of telling Linda."

Twenty minutes later, Manny hung up his office phone after talking with Susan. She and the kids jumped up and down, screaming with delight. Ryan asked, "What does podnah mean?"

Manny glanced at the painting of the sunrise over his couch and smiled. He got up from his desk as he sent off a text message to Noah:

Gather the troops.
Time to celebrate.
Details soon.

He walked down the hallway and saw Rachel hiding her liquid afternoon pick-me-up. "Caught ya!!" he said, smiling.

Rachel gave a big old grin as she slid her canteen into the drawer. "Breath mint?" she replied nervously. But Manny kept on walking. He reached Linda's door and saw her staring into her computer, working on a spreadsheet. He knocked softly on the doorpost. "Have a minute for some good news?"

Linda looked up with a smile.

Over eight million souls vibrated in the City of New York that afternoon. Manny Johnson was one of them.

The vibation was epic.

PART SEVEN

❖   ❖   ❖

Final Items

ABOUT THE AUTHOR

Ray East is an author, speaker and executive leadership coach. Through his company, Horizon East, he's helped many talented leaders learn what it takes to achieve breakthrough results through other people. He serves individuals and teams by providing coaching, workshops, strategic planning retreats and conferences.

Ray is a former Fortune-500 executive and international corporate attorney. His career has granted him many opportunities to lead teams, including overseas teams when he led several investigative missions as a pro-bono attorney for the International Justice Mission. He holds a J.D. from Columbia University, an M.A. in International Relations from The Johns Hopkins University and a B.A. from Vassar College.

Ray is currently enjoying the adventure of living with a purpose in New York City, surrounded by a community of friends.

You can learn more about Ray or invite him to speak at your event by visiting RayEast.com

WHY I WROTE THE STORY

At some point today, you probably tried to influence someone. If you were successful in influencing the person, that means you led them; you got a result from them. Leadership is the art of achieving results through other human beings.

It's important to note that leadership is not something that only movie heroes, corporate executives and presidents do. It's something that *you* do every day. Perhaps you are a stay-at-home mom. Maybe you are a CEO. Either way, if you regularly try to influence people then please know that you are a leader.

Once I developed the eyes to see it, I saw leadership making a difference everywhere. It's the fuel that makes our families, businesses, nonprofits and governments run properly. But once I started to realize leadership's significance to our world, a pesky question came to mind: if leading is such a crucial dynamic, then why do so few people do it well? Vast numbers of people seem unaware of what's at the core of being a good leader. What is the core?

I really wanted to know the answer because, while I've had some remarkably good bosses over the years, I've also been burned a few times by well-intentioned people who neglected to lead well. I followed their lead because I had to, not because I wanted to. Even though I set my mind to accomplish the tasks they gave me, all along, I wanted to give my heart too.

These leaders didn't understand the core of good leadership; they never learned the reason why people follow a leader. They practiced a bewildering amount of management techniques on me, but they failed to move me. They never inspired me to invest my whole self.

When I first started leading teams, I was surprised to find that I too was unable to provide my followers with the very inspiration that I craved. This troubled me. How could someone like me, who was willing to do whatever it took to lead well, end up being ineffective as a leader? That's when I started the quest to identify that crucial, missing core that makes someone a brilliant leader.

Over the years, I tried to keep my eyes open as I led teams and coached leaders in the business and nonprofit sectors. Eventually, I bumped into the unlikely insight that Life was the missing aspect. The primary reason that people follow a leader is to experience Life, with "Life" defined broadly as a person's optimal state of being.

In the countless workplaces that I've seen, what most people long for most has little to do with getting a higher salary, more power or a fancier title. Those things are all nice, but what workers most need is a change in the selfish and fearful ways that the people in their workplaces relate to each other. They need to experience real Life at work if they are going to achieve difficult breakthroughs and sustain high performance forever.

This is why we need to raise a generation of Life-giving leaders who can transform dysfunctional corporate cultures into atmospheres of purpose, adventure and community. This beautiful context of Life is the only context in which breakthrough performance can endure.

But how exactly do you invite Life to show up in your team dynamics? In time, I started noticing in offices that the most healthy and productive teams had leaders who got one thing right: they were soft when needed, and strong when required. They were humble and considerate on one hand and yet bold and tenacious on the other. They seemed comfortable leading from either extreme, and significantly, they could discern when the time was right to operate from each end of the spectrum. This stood in stark contrast to the familiar situation in which a boss often acts like an abusive bully or a wimpy pushover because that was the way they were predisposed. Instead of acting how they

were "predisposed" to act, the effective leaders had trained themselves over time to adjust their displays of power and restraint in
each situation to encourage a spirit of community, purpose and
adventure. Amazing, I thought.

These observations led me to conclude that confident humility is what makes an atmosphere of Life happen. When a leader
intentionally has her strength under control in a way that
generates Life, she can yield never-ending results from her team.

I've witnessed in myself and others that confidence without
humility is arrogance. I've also seen that humility without confidence is insecurity. Neither arrogance nor insecurity is becoming
in a leader. It makes sense that a confident style of humility is
required to captivate the hearts and minds of people on a mission.

In my leadership coaching practice, I observed that organizational breakthroughs routinely happened when my clients were
willing to do two things: give sacrificially to make their teams
succeed, and; empower their people to see themselves as leaders
as they accomplished their mission. Since both actions require
great self-confidence and humility, I concluded that building
a culture of sustained high performance is something that only
confident and humble leaders can do.

I've observed that a little confident humility leads to just
a little Life in a team. On the other hand, lots of confident humility leads to abundant Life. This correlation is true at home, in the
office or anywhere else on the planet.

The great leaders in history practiced the art of inspiring
Life-giving, results-oriented communities. South Africa provides
an example of what is possible when a great leader remembers
and practices strength under control for the benefit of Life.
Prisoner Nelson Mandela had to exercise great humility to emerge
from his decades of incarceration unoffended. He had to muster
a fierce resolve to forgive his oppressors. But it was precisely this
strong but forgiving character that gave President Mandela the
credibility and moral right to lead the South African people into

an unprecedented period of democracy and national healing. His many sacrificial efforts, empowered by confident humility, were a major factor in the genesis of a national forgiveness movement that was ultimately embodied by the Truth and Reconciliation Commission. Much bloodshed was avoided by this wave of Life. And the success was directly attributable to the confident humility of Nelson Mandela and the people of South Africa. I've learned from the example of several great leaders in history that strength under control is the most powerful force for change on earth.

Imagine my surprise one day when I read Jim Collins's findings in his powerful book *Good To Great*. According to his empirical research, there is a unique profile of a leader who can take a Fortune 500 corporation from good to great. The raw numbers revealed a truth that Jim Collins admitted he didn't see coming beforehand: only leaders who possessed deep humility and fierce resolve could successfully transform a company from good to great.

There it was. My mouth dropped open as I saw my personal observations confirmed by empirical data. Moreover, Collins's measure of a company's greatness was measured by—get this—annual profits earned over a fifteen-year period. Not employee work-life balance survey results, but cold, hard cash.

Once I realized that confident humility was a decisive factor in whether companies could make cash, that was all I needed to know. I recognized that I was onto something that was measurable, financial and real, and I wanted decision makers to explore this underappreciated kind of leadership with me.

So that's why I wrote *The Life of Manny*. I wanted to give everyone a very practical vision of what confident humility could look like when lived out in a workplace. I wanted you to see the monetary, physical, mental, emotional and spiritual Life that this blended trait can bring.

Human beings can achieve almost anything they can visualize in their mind's eye. I am hoping that people like you will set your sights on this particular vision of Life, then change the world, one home, office or classroom at a time. A good way to start might be to begin a discussion group on Life-giving leadership in your office, home or religious community. Be sure to visit TheLifeofManny.com or ConfidentHumility.com if you'd like to learn about additional resources to help you.

I have more leadership concepts that I'd like to explore with you, but they will have to wait until my next book.

And speaking of books, thank you for reading this one.

Ray East
May 5, 2009
New York City

HOW YOU CAN SHARE THE STORY

A group of us who have benefitted from reading *The Life of Manny* want to see our wider communities benefit from this book too. Not only is the story a fun read, but the confident humility content has the power to transform thousands of dark workplaces into Life-giving environments.

If you too have enjoyed learning from the book, please help us create the word of mouth needed to make a difference. Word of mouth is the best way to get this book into enough hands to transform our wider community.

You may already have thought of some creative ways to get the word out. If not, here are some suggestions that may help:

- Pick up a few copies of the book and give them to your friends, your boss, your team, your pastor, your reading group, college students or anyone else who could benefit from Manny's wisdom. The book provides an easy-to-read story that gives leaders the inspiration and practical wisdom they'll need to get results and transform their teams.

- For those of you with blogs or websites, write about how the book made a difference in the way you do Life and leadership. Recommend *The Life of Manny* and provide a link to http://www.The**Life**of**Manny**.com

- Contact television programs, radio shows or podcasts, and request that the author be interviewed as a guest on the show. The media is often much more responsive to their audience than to requests from publicists.

- Think about writing your own review of the book and submitting it to a magazine, newspaper or website.

- If you're a storeowner, consider displaying *The Life of Manny* on your countertop. The book is offered at a discounted rate for resellers who order multiple copies.

- Give a set of books to a college library, inner city school, rehabilitation house, prison or any other community that may be looking for Life. In every group, there are always emerging leaders who would love to learn how to transform their community.

- If you've found any typos or errors while reading this book, won't you please help us and future readers by sending an email citing the problem and the appropriate page number to typos@TheLifeofManny.com. We really appreciate your help.

If you want to learn more about how invest in a generation of Life-giving leaders or how to create an atmosphere of purpose, adventure and community, please visit the website:

TheLifeofManny.com

And thank you for helping us.

❖   ❖   ❖

ACKNOWLEDGMENTS

Since *The Life of Manny* was my first book, some of the demands in the writing and publishing process took me by surprise. Many aspects took longer than I imagined and required more effort than I expected. I needed lots of help. Many generous people gave their time, talent, wisdom and inspiration to make this book happen. I was sincerely touched by the selfless contributions of my friends, colleagues and family members. Thank you all. Please forgive me if I forgot to mention you here by name.

Mamacita Margarita, you have influenced me in profound ways that defy description. You inspired a foundation of love in my life. Thank you for sustaining me in so many ways while I created this book. I couldn't have done this without you. Thank you for being my biggest encourager.

Calixto and Gian: a million fun times come to mind. I am so grateful that I got to be in the same family with you and learn from you. Thank you for being there for me.

To Cyranna L. Love, Zion J. Spencer and Peter C. Han, my first round of readers and my circle of strength: thank you, marvelous comrades, for helping me know that I was on the right track. Your countless hours of editing, proofing, encouraging and praying made the difference. I'm glad you were the first ones to help shape the drafts. Your investment in this project was deeply significant. And, as you all know, parts of you ended up in me, which, in turn, ended up in the book. So thank you.

To my friends at Trinity Grace Church: a colossal thank you to Suzanne Erickson, Jon Tyson, Edward Huang, Joshua Staton, Gary Wiley and Alf Bishai. Your contributions raised the bar in substantial ways. I couldn't imagine releasing the book without your powerful feedback. And Sue, you went far beyond the call of duty… twice! I am amazed at how sharp and talented you are. Thank you for lending me your smarts for a while.

At The King's College: I owe a huge debt of gratitude to Eric Bennett, David Leedy, Shelli Cline, Noah Hunter, Steven Arnold, and James Nordby. Your helpful manuscript comments and conversations about leadership were a Godsend.

Gabrien and Rusan Symons, you provided early encouragement and loads of logistical help just when I needed it. You also helped me to dream in the right direction. My gratitude goes to you and to the entire Friday Fellowship Group who supported me in countless ways through this process.

Brian, Jennifer, Madeleine and Cora Milner: thank you for letting me turn your basement into Ray's writing laboratory for a long season. I really enjoyed your company and your airbed too.

To my editor Mary Loebig-Giles: your insights strengthened the work and gave me confidence that the book was ready for public consumption. Thank you.

To Karrie Ross, who designed the book cover and interior layout: thank you for working with my changing timelines, making my book beautiful, and having a joyful outlook on life.

To my executive coaching clients, former bosses and business acquaintances throughout the years: thank you for showing me what good leadership was all about.

And to the Manny's and Linda's everywhere: Thanks for being who you are. Turn up the volume a little more every day.

❖   ❖   ❖

LINDA'S NOTES ON LEADERSHIP

Concepts from Chapter Five:

- A leader makes Life happen for herself and her people because Life is the only context that can sustain high performance forever.

- Definition of Life: a person's optimal state of being (real life begins once all your basic needs are met—when you're thriving, not just surviving).

- People encounter Life at work as they find their purpose, dive into an adventure, connect with community and create results.

- A wise leader moves her company forward by using the knowledge that her people will always do whatever they think will bring them the most Life.

- If you turn work into an opportunity to find Life, your people will dive into work with more passion and generate better results.

- If you get the one thing (Life) right, when you mess up, people will still follow you.

- As a leader protects and advances the Life of her people, she empowers them to make breakthrough results happen. It's so simple that it's easy to forget. So remember: real leadership brings Life, which in turn makes breakthroughs happen.

- Life is what makes a leader attractive to people. People give their loyalty to leaders who consistently provide Life.

- You can tinker with leadership tips and techniques forever, but you'll never accomplish anything significant through your team until you choose to make Life happen for your people and your mission.

- Some executives derail their careers by not knowing how to use the correct tools at the correct time. Sometimes they keep their leadership positions, but end up failing at Life. They stay in their jobs only because their companies are too shortsighted to care that they are poor leaders.

- So how do you know which leadership skills to apply in a given situation? Simply think about Life when you reach into the toolbox. Ask yourself, "How can I use my skills to create the most Life in this situation?"

Concepts from Chapter Eight:

- Bring your best practices from home to create Life at work.

- The leader at home and the leader at work may use different behaviors, but they must have identical motives: to make Life happen.

- Distinguish yourself as one who has ambition for the Life of your organization, and not yourself. You experience Life as you give it to others, so you don't have to look out for yourself as much as you'd think.

- Regardless of your background, everyone can and must be a student of Life. Observe the healthy relationships around you for signs of Life. Do the work of finding out why Life is showing up in those contexts.

- Life happens when your people know they matter and you're on their side.

- Constantly plant seeds of inclusion with your words and, more importantly, your actions.

- Empower your people to see themselves as leaders who are responsible for making sure the right things happen when they execute their mission.

Concepts from Chapter Ten:

- When you're promoted from an individual contributor to a leader, a conversion has to happen in your thinking: although you've always learned to win by personally standing out, now the way to win is to make your team's performance stand out.

- People spend a long time trying to break in a new baseball glove so that it works better. In the same way, a leader must be broken in to sustainably create powerful results through human assistants. The breaking-in process is designed to impart confident humility (steel and velvet) into a leader so she can make Life happen.

- Compelling leaders blend steel and velvet virtues to secure the superior team results that only come from devotion. What devotion? The followers' devotion to their mission, to each other and to their leader.

- Some of the best leaders are introverts. It doesn't matter if your style is introverted or extroverted (Life requires all types of leaders). The only thing that matters is that your leadership style has been broken in with confident humility.

Concepts from Chapter Eleven:

- A broken-in leader makes Life happen by demonstrating confidence and humility. But humility is a far more compelling concept than most people realize.

- Humility is the state of being so comfortable with yourself that no selfless task is beneath you. Do the hard work of learning how valuable you really are until you don't have to use your activities to prove your importance. You're on the right track when your emotions start to grasp that you have nothing to lose by taking humble actions. That's how you know you're a well-grounded person.

- Humility doesn't mean thinking less of yourself; it means thinking of yourself less often because you're already in touch with your immeasurable worth.

- Increasing your understanding of your self-worth is not selfish; it's actually the most secure basis for serving others selflessly. Don't avoid growing your self-worth because you're afraid you'll grow arrogant (that's false humility). You'll be fine as long as you (1) seek to know your great worth at the *heart* level as well as intellectually; and (2) increase your understanding of *other people's* worth as well as your own.

- When you have nothing left to prove, you can afford to invest in the person in front of you rather than watching out for yourself all the time (which is so boring).

- Life requires leaders to rely on vast reserves of accurate self-worth. Pursuing this heart-level experience is a journey. We're not designed to make the journey alone. Surround yourself with fearless, humble, Life-filled mentors and friends who can help you see yourself as you truly are. Also, using a Life coach, a pastor or a counselor may be a good idea.

Concepts from Chapter Twelve:

The Breaking-In Process of a Leader (How to make daily decisions)

    1. Discover how Life wants to show up right now.

    2. Invent an action plan to make that Life happen.

    3. Execute the plan with confident humility.

Then learn from your success and mistakes, go back to step one, and do it again.

- The core of being a good leader is intentionally having your strength under control in a way that generates Life (confident humility).

- When people trust you to take their interests into consideration along with your own, it unlocks their hearts and releases them to be selfless in pursuing the team's strategy. That's how you sustain a culture of breakthroughs.

- Breaking in a stallion has to do with a saddle and harness. Breaking in a leader has to do with developing your choices, emotions and thoughts so that you become aligned with Life. The end result is that you know how to intentionally measure your displays of power and restraint in every situation to encourage community, purpose and adventure in the people around you.

- All humans have a rider. Some of us serve the purposes of Life and some serve Self-Concern.

- Two dynamics happen simultaneously when a leader is being broken in: First, the selfish, impulsive side of the leader's will starts to disappear. At the same time, a mature character emerges and the leader's strengths are brought under control. As a result, the leader begins to rise above self-concern.

- People may sometimes misinterpret your confident humility as a sign of weakness. But it usually works to your advantage when people underestimate the reach of your inner intensity.

Concepts from Chapter Seventeen:

- Life is not for wimps. Life demands results from leaders in two realms: the Life of the people on your team, and the Life produced when your team achieves its mission well. Your team's mission represents the Life of your stakeholders, including your customers, colleagues, bosses, investors, vendors and community.

- A leader has to make sure that Life is showing up in <u>both</u> realms at all times by using confident humility.

- Keeping your eyes on both realms of Life may seem like an obvious priority, but you'd be surprised how often leaders neglect one realm or the other. Neglecting either one will have serious consequences for your stakeholders.

- Don't give in to believing that you're forced to harm either your people or your results. When you learn how to lead creatively, very rarely will you be forced to choose between your people and your mission. This is why it's so important for us to be broken in. We need to discover the ways that Life can show up in both realms.

Concepts from Chapter Eighteen:

- Every time you act with confident humility, you make an impact. Life always flows from confident and humble leadership.

- I never knew that leading by making Life happen for

other people could make me feel so alive! This is what I was born for. Mama would be proud!

"Let us put our minds together and
see what Life we can make for our children."
—Sitting Bull

ORDERING THIS BOOK

If you would like to order copies of this book,
please visit the website:

www.The**Life**of**Manny**.com

THANK YOU

If you've found any typos or errors while reading this book,
won't you please help us and future readers
by sending an email citing the problem and the
appropriate page number to typos@TheLifeofManny.com.
We really appreciate your help.